More praise for *Human Resources in the Family Business*

"Family-owned businesses have always been and will continue to be important drivers of the economy. This book, *Human Resources in the Family Business*, provides the tools to select, develop, and deploy employees so company results are maximized."
—Gerald L. Shaheen, Retired Group President, Caterpillar Inc.; Director, AGCO Corporation, FORD Motor Company

"Valuable and transformative insights for families and professionals of family enterprises. Those moving from either family or business to family and business will greatly benefit from this book."
—James A. Burton, Chairman, PPI; Board Member, Institute for Family Advisors

"Besides being an excellent technical resource for general HR management, Ransburg, Sage-Hayward, and Schuman have provided compelling evidence and impactful tools for families in business to not just manage, but also leverage their unique human resource dynamics. A must-read for any family-controlled enterprise!"
—Allen S. Taylor, Chair, Canadian Association of Family Enterprise (CAFE)

"I have come to appreciate Amy Schuman as a friend and as a fantastic resource in family business for more than ten years. As I read *Human Resources in the Family Business*, I saw what an HR playbook, not only for family businesses, but a playbook for HR departments in any organization can look like. Its step-by-step look into the fundamentals of a successful HR partnership with family or business leaders provides great guidance. There are numerous examples and worksheets to help HR professionals create their own processes and stories of success. You will enjoy reading and applying what the authors have laid out for all of us."
—Vince Newendorp, VP & Chief Administration Officer, Vermeer

"From recruiting and onboarding to culture and exit, *Human Resources in the Family Business* guides readers through the intricacies of human resources in family firms. Filled with practical tools, this is a text that will inspire family businesses to persistently reach for more."
—Judi Cunningham, Family Enterprise Advisor and Founder of the Institute of Family Enterprise Advisors

"Whether your family business has an actual HR department or not, this book is a must-read for any family business leader—family member or not—who wants to maximize the contribution of their people. Not only will it help you take a more strategic view of human resources, but it is also filled with practical tips that you can start using right away."
—Andrew Libman, Director and President of The Libman Company

Human Resources in the Family Business

A FAMILY——
BUSINESS
——PUBLICATION

Family Business Publications are the combined efforts of the Family Business Consulting Group and Palgrave Macmillan. These books provide useful information on a broad range of topics that concern the family business enterprise, including succession planning, communication, strategy and growth, family leadership, and more. The books are written by experts with combined experiences of over a century in the field of family enterprise and who have consulted with thousands of enterprising families the world over, giving the reader practical, effective, and time-tested insights to everyone involved in a family business.

The Family Business Consulting Group, Inc., founded in 1994, is the leading business consultancy exclusively devoted to helping family enterprises prosper across generations.

Human Resources in the Family Business

Maximizing the Power of Your People

David Ransburg, Wendy Sage-Hayward, and
Amy M. Schuman

HUMAN RESOURCES IN THE FAMILY BUSINESS
Copyright © David Ransburg, Wendy Sage-Hayward, and Amy M. Schuman 2016

First published 2016 by
PALGRAVE MACMILLAN

The authors have asserted their rights to be identified as the authors of this work in accordance with the Copyright, Designs and Patents Act 1988.

Palgrave Macmillan in the UK is an imprint of Macmillan Publishers Limited, registered in England, company number 785998, of Houndmills, Basingstoke, Hampshire, RG21 6XS.

Palgrave Macmillan in the US is a division of Nature America, Inc., One New York Plaza, Suite 4500, New York, NY 10004-1562.

Palgrave Macmillan is the global academic imprint of the above companies and has companies and representatives throughout the world.

Hardback ISBN: 978–1–137–44426–4
E-PUB ISBN: 978–1–137–44428–8
E-PDF ISBN: 978–1–137–44427–1
DOI: 10.1057/9781137444271

Distribution in the UK, Europe and the rest of the world is by Palgrave Macmillan®, a division of Macmillan Publishers Limited, registered in England, company number 785998, of Houndmills, Basingstoke, Hampshire RG21 6XS.

Library of Congress Cataloging-in-Publication Data

Ransburg, David.
    Human resources in the family business : maximizing the power of your people / David Ransburg, Wendy Sage-Hayward, Amy M. Schuman.
      pages cm
    Includes index.
    ISBN 978–1–137–44426–4 (alk. paper)
     1. Family-owned business enterprises—Management. 2. Personnel management. I. Sage-Hayward, Wendy, II. Schuman, Amy M. III. Title.

HD62.25.R3566 2015
658.3—dc23   2015018299

A catalogue record of the book is available from the British Library.

Printed in the United States of America.

Amy
For my colleagues at The Family Business Consulting Group, who inspire me every day with their humility, curiosity and creativity.

David
For my family, who defines me.

Wendy
To all of our clients over the years who have opened up their hearts and minds to us. We would have no expertise to share without you.

Contents

Figures

Tables

Preface

We wrote this book for a simple reason: we saw a great need to help family businesses address the many challenges and opportunities they face in relation to managing their human resources (HR). A strong, well-supported HR function in any organization provides tremendous benefits to individual contributors as well as to the broader organization. Part of the challenge is that managing HR in any family business involves multiple, complex, interrelated issues with many nuances. Just a small sample of HR questions for family businesses include the following:

- How do you employ family members in the business in a way that works best for the family, the business, and the individuals?
- How do you identify, interview, and hire the best people among both family and nonfamily members?
- How do you develop individual and firm-level capabilities that ensure constant evolution of every kind?
- How do you deal with tricky HR issues related to sensitive topics such as underperforming family employees?
- How do you manage employee exits effectively, especially those of family members?
- How does the HR function—in whatever form it takes—interface with the family? How is this group's role with the family best carried out?
- How does the HR function lead and contribute to the business's culture?

Answering these and many other questions thoughtfully is an important challenge for the family business, as the decisions made will influence the firm's culture and performance. People—and how they are treated—are the foundation a family business because it is the company's people who help create the infrastructure that will enable a business to live past any individual founder. In this book we have articulated HR challenges in family businesses and presented strategies, frameworks, and tools for managing these effectively. We firmly believe this highly complex set of issues can be broken down into manageable tasks and fulfilled, with excellence, by any family business.

Part of our inspiration for writing this book is that our previous corporate and consulting work has brought us into contact with many executives and managers, within and outside formal HR departments, who are struggling to manage HR issues. We hope this book will help them learn from one another and from us, especially from the stories and examples of how family firms and others across market sectors have handled their own HR challenges.

That brings us to an important question: why are we the right people to write this book? Together, we have nearly a century of experience in different sectors including agriculture, automotive, consumer products, construction, financial services, health care/insurance, manufacturing, real estate, retail (in multiple forms), technology, tourism, and others. We have served well over 200 organizations as trusted advisers, both before and during our tenures as consultants with the Family Business Consulting Group ("FBCG"), a Chicago-based business founded in 1994 to help family enterprises prosper across generations.

Our experience as individual professionals, including both "in-house" and consulting roles related directly or indirectly to human resources issues, informs everything in this book:

- Amy Schuman served as Director of Organizational Development for 12 years with Fel-Pro, a family-owned maker of automotive gaskets and sealants that was eventually acquired by Federal Mogul. As a key nonfamily executive, Amy was present during the transition from the second to the third generation and helped support the firm's cultural transformation from paternalistic to performance centered, emphasizing employee participation and a strong sense of ownership at every level, including team-based manufacturing processes and compensation. Such features helped Fel-Pro earn a place in Fortune's Top 10 Best Companies to Work for in America, among other honors. Amy was the founding facilitator and coach in the Next Generation Leadership Institute at the Loyola University Chicago Family Business Center, a one-of-a-kind leadership training program that helps fast-rising family business leaders fully realize their leadership potential. She has written multiple books on family business issues.

- Wendy Sage-Hayward has extensive experience working on human capital issues. She has worked as an organizational-development consultant for over 26 years, covering a variety of topics related to the development and management of HR. That has meant partnering regularly with HR departments of firms and nondepartment-based HR functions across sectors to develop and implement initiatives related to strategic planning, training and development, performance management, executive coaching, and many other areas—always with a focus on positioning HR as a strategic partner within the organization. Wendy is also an adjunct professor at the University of British Columbia's Sauder School of Business, where she teaches families and their professional advisers to address the complexity and challenges associated with the human factor in family business, whether leadership development, ownership development, governance, or succession. Additionally, Wendy is an owner and director of a six-generation, 130-year-old agricultural family business with 45 family partners.

- David Ransburg has also served in multiple corporate and consulting roles, with the additional dimension of experience in psychology. He was an owner, manager, and board member with his family's consumer-products manufacturing business, working on key initiatives including the sale of the company to German multinational Bosch. David also served as a consultant with leading independent benefits compensation and HR consultancy Sibson, along with working in corporate finance at LaSalle Partners (now Jones Lang LaSalle) and as a staff therapist with Northwestern University's Family Institute. He has also served as faculty for Northwestern University and Loyola University, with a focus on family business leadership issues.

As FBCG consultants, each of us is involved deeply in our clients' human resources issues, helping them diagnose issues and develop high-value plans, programs, strategies, and solutions. These include issues related to leadership transitions, continuity, identification and development of family/non family talent, executive assessment, compensation, family employment policies, mentoring, career development, communication between and among family and nonfamily managers and employees, management of relationships and dynamics, family conflict/psychology issues (such as divorce and addiction), and many others.

We are excited to share with you key insights we've gained from our continued, ever-evolving experience with human resources issues in family-owned and other organizations.

Acknowledgments

First and foremost, we would like to thank our many client families. Our clients inspire us every day, and have fostered our desire to share our learning with you in this book. We are deeply appreciative for the thoughtful approaches of our clients to the human resource function—each one slightly different, but all reflecting great care and creativity. By sharing their journeys with us in ways large and small, our clients enabled us to develop and enrich so much of the material contained in this book.

We are especially thankful to those clients who allowed us to interview them for this book and include their stories as illustrations of excellent human resource practices in family business. These include Kathryn Bader and Martha Jahn Martin; Anna Ball from Ball Horticultural; Jeremy Baude and Rodney Benson from Danica; Ken Chaun from Kal Tire; John McHugh from Kwik Trip; Bill Phelps, Will Phelps, and Elizabeth Neuman from Joseph Phelps Vineyards; Todd Plymate from Plymate, Inc.; and Jeff Vincent from Laird Norton Company.

We are also extremely grateful to Sachin Waikar, who guided us through this journey with patience, perseverance, and a gentle but firm grasp on our collective hand, which kept us moving forward—especially at times when our momentum waned or we became distracted due to workload or other important life events (like one of us becoming a grandparent!). We also want to thank Michael Mok for his assistance in making our diagrams look distinct and professional.

We are grateful to our colleagues at the Family Business Consulting Group, who have been gracious and generous in sharing their knowledge and insights with us in our work with family businesses. A special thank you to Anne Hargrave, who painstakingly reviewed each chapter and provided valuable feedback despite her heavy workload.

We wish to thank Laurie Harting at Palgrave Macmillan, who from the start encouraged us to write this book and provided ongoing support that invested us with just the right dose of excitement and inspiration to carry on.

Finally, we would also like to thank our families for their patience and generosity in giving us the time and space to work on this project over the past year and a half. Without their support, encouragement and love we would never have been able to complete this book.

1

Introduction

As we see it, HR is truly the beating heart of your business, as it is all about enhancing the experience, engagement, and performance of what is considered the most valuable asset of most companies: your people. Yet because HR is often overlooked, we want to highlight its importance in the family business with three mutually reinforcing points.

People matter, so HR matters to any business, especially family firms. We are not the only ones to point out the criticality of HR in business. Others have noted how HR matters because people matter—more in the context of business today than ever before. Firms with an actively engaged workforce report 2.6 times the growth in earnings per share than counterparts with disengaged employees.[1] In fact, over 30 studies have correlated employee engagement to variables including better sales, profits, productivity, and customer service, along with decreases in turnover, absenteeism, product defects, and safety incidents.[2] While HR might seem like a relatively "easy" business function, creating thoughtful systems that maximize engagement, productivity, and satisfaction is far from easy, and requires a strategic approach to both the crafting of HR practices and their implementation.

We suggest that HR is even more important in family business for the following reasons: ,

- *Family firms often treat employees—whether family or nonfamily—as family,* thus putting more attention and pressure on the need to handle HR issues with great care and respect.

- *Family dynamics complicate the emotional environment of a family business—for better and sometimes for worse.* The inclusion of family employees in many family businesses mandates a careful approach to HR issues at every stage of the HR life cycle, from recruiting to exit. That is, it is hard enough to deal with hiring/firing and development of nonfamily employees, so handling such issues strategically and sensitively with family employees is paramount.
- *Family relationships and the family's reputation are at stake, which is a huge risk for the family and the business.* When HR issues are dealt with poorly in the business they have an impact on the family system—which can have devastating effects. We have seen families where estrangement and lawsuits are the result of poorly managed HR challenges in the family firm.
- *The livelihoods and fortunes of business families are often tied up in the enterprises they run,* so they need to maximize the value of the business, including getting HR right on every dimension so their income source remains intact.

Family firms outperform nonfamily firms—and this is correlated with how they manage HR. There is a substantial, growing body of evidence for the superior returns and sustainability of family firms compared to nonfamily businesses across dimensions. One study found that family enterprises outperformed the S&P 500 by up to 15 percent over a ten-year period.[3] Research on Canadian firms has shown that family firms outpaced nonfamily businesses significantly on share price from 1998 to 2012.[4] A *Harvard Business Review* article highlighted extensive evidence from the United States, Canada, and Europe that family businesses outperform their nonfamily peers during adverse economic times.[5] To study outcomes beyond financial performance, another research group compared hundreds of family-controlled and nonfamily-controlled public businesses and found that family-owned firms implement more employee- and community-focused social initiatives.[6] Moreover, family firms are viewed as exemplars of long-term thinking, which helps them avoid overfocusing on near-term results and manage risk, liquidity, and other factors with a longer time horizon in mind. That approach contributes to greater returns and longevity.[7]

Because your business's performance is so highly dependent on your people, HR is a crucial contributor to the superior performance of your family firm. So maximizing the effectiveness of your HR systems and practices will help maximize your performance across the board.

HR can and should be a strategic partner within the firm, rather than just a transaction-focused administrative function. As mentioned earlier, despite the potential value of HR, too many firms fail to use this function strategically, relegating it to an administrative and/ or policing role, with a focus on the nuts and bolts of the employee experience or the perfunctory enforcement of routine policies. As such, HR becomes more like a metaphorical finger-wagging librarian than a trusted, value-generating partner. These firms are missing out on potentially larger opportunities for creating value on multiple dimensions—or at the very least for involving HR when dealing with complex employee-related and cultural issues. There is mounting evidence for the strategic value of HR—both the people and the systems/ processes involved. One piece is the rise of the CHRO, or chief human resources officer. A recent *Harvard Business Review* article notes that HR leaders at many firms now report directly to the CEO (rather than the COO or CFO) and serve as key advisers to the top executive and board, requiring higher-level leadership and strategy skills.[8] The article's title sums up the newfound appreciation for the power of HR: "Why Chief Human Resources Officers Make Great CEOs."

We believe strongly that HR can be an enabler rather than a disabler, a builder rather than a blockade, a partner rather than a peripheral player. In short, the ideal role for HR is as a true champion of engagement of *all* firm resources, not just the human ones. In many firms that will mean taking clear, practical steps to transition HR into a more strategic role. We wrote this book to help you do exactly that.

More specifically, we want to help you address questions like these:

- How do you identify candidates for employment who align best with the underlying culture and values of your family business—and how do you convey your attractiveness to them as a desirable place to work?

- How can you choose from well-qualified interviewees, each bringing a range of appealing experience within and outside family business?
- What is the best way to introduce a new hire to the rest of the business, and communicate their arrival, especially when the person in question is a member of the owning family?
- How can you bring people into the business in a way that ensures they and the company benefit most?
- What tricky issues might you encounter in reviewing the performance of family employees, and what is the best way to handle these issues?
- How do you develop and promote leadership within the family while simultaneously keeping high-potential nonfamily employees engaged, motivated, and committed to your business?
- How can you best anticipate and manage the departure of employees—both family and nonfamily—from the business, being mindful of issues including possible re-entry and repercussions?

HR as a Missed Opportunity

If you're reading this book, you probably already appreciate the importance of HR in family business. But the reality is that while many firms think strategically about their products, services, competition, marketing, and other traditional business areas, they do not apply the same rigor to HR management, thus missing powerful opportunities to create value on many different levels. As family business consultants with many decades of experience collectively, we often see large, untapped opportunities to make more strategic and effective use of HR for the benefit of the business, the family, and the employees. A comprehensive and well-planned approach to HR will clearly position your business with a strategic advantage and simultaneously help your people get the most out of their careers.

We recognize that HR management is a truly complex issue for family firms. There are many overlapping dimensions and layers of complexity to navigate due to the integration of family, business, and ownership, in contrast to nonfamily firms. The resources to help families and family-business executives manage HR issues can be few, far between, and fragmented. We have seen no other book that brings together thinking on HR practices in family firms as we do in this book. Our goal is to raise awareness of key HR issues and provide practical examples, frameworks, tools, and tips you can apply within your family business that result in real change—all as components of an overarching, dynamic model of HR in the family business.

How We Define Family Business and Human Resources

Before we dive further into the topic of HR in family business, it is important to define key terms as we will use them in this book.[9] First, *family business*. We think of family business as the following:

1. Any business in which the family has effective control over the strategic direction of the business, *and* in which the business contributes significantly to the family's wealth, income, or identity.
2. The family has control over the business and ownership, and intends to pass the business to future generations.
3. Multiple members of the same family are involved as major owners or managers, either simultaneously or sequentially over time.

Second, *HR*. The conventional definition of HR is the variety of activities required to manage employees and employee-related policies and practices in a business.[10] That definition of HR includes the professionals who practice it, along with the associated practices, procedures, and paperwork (including the virtual kind). We prefer a broad view of HR that includes all activities related to the HR "life cycle" within a company, along with the values-based cultural features that inform every stage of the life cycle. As discussed in more detail in the "Our Model" chapter, the stages included in the life cycle are the following (see Figure 1.1):

- *Recruiting*: How and where to find the best pool of potential employees both within and outside the family.
- *Selection*: How to choose the optimal employees to hire among viable candidates, especially when owning family members are involved.

- *Onboarding*: How to transition new hires into the company to ensure an effective integration for the new employees, the company, and the family.
- *Development*: How to sensitively manage the review and development of family and nonfamily employees with a focus on continually improving the business's ability to develop its people.
- *Exit*: How to develop a process that helps employees depart from the company in the most mutually beneficial way, whether the exit is voluntary or involuntary, and whether the individual is likely to return to the business in the future or not. In addition, how to prevent the exit of a family member from the business from becoming an exit from the family.

As noted above, we also consider *culture* an important aspect of HR, as it expresses the family's values in the business and informs all components of the HR life cycle, including how and where you look for new employees (and the qualifications you seek in them), how you bring them into the business, and how you align their behaviors with the business's values and strategy through onboarding,

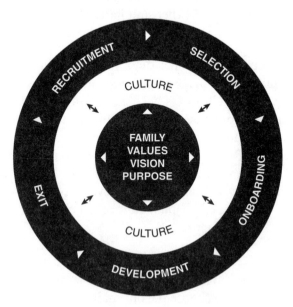

Figure 1.1   Our model of HR in family business.

development, and other processes. The "Culture" chapter considers these and related topics in depth.

For our purposes, the idea of talking about "HR staff" is also too narrow, as it relates only to those professionals housed within a formal HR department. Again, we prefer a broad definition that focuses not so much on titles but roles. *Anyone* who is part of an HR effort will be considered part of a firm's HR processes for our purposes. One example is how, in many retail businesses (family-owned in particular), store managers, though not formally part of the HR organization, play a large role in the majority of HR activities reflected in the life cycle stages above: hiring, training, development, and exit, among others. In fact, we believe all managers, across industries and functions, should consider their role to include HR elements, as part of a culture of deep collaboration.

So HR, as used here, will mean the functions, people, knowledge, and practices aimed at linking the human talent within the business with the highest possible levels of performance and satisfaction not only for employees but also for other stakeholders, including customers and the family shareholders. We will try to clarify when we are using "HR" to refer to specific management practices or tools versus the role of an HR professional or group, but we trust you to understand which meaning is intended based on the context, as well.

Embrace the "Both-And" Mindset

The family or the business?

That is a choice many business-owning families and family business executives feel they have to make: which of those to prioritize over the other? This question is often directly related to HR policies and practices. Generally, do HR decisions tend to favor the business or the family? For example, are hiring criteria relaxed when hiring family members, or are higher levels of qualification and experience made mandatory?

The family-or-business question is the *wrong* question to ask. It is not an "either-or" approach but a "both-and" mindset. We believe in finding approaches that are best for the business *and* the family. There is a growing school of thought on the power of paradox in family business. This approach sees the most successful family firms as having a well-developed capability to embrace paradox, turning each "either-or" into a "both-and," rather than avoiding the issue and crafting suboptimal compromises.[11] This "both-and" approach can be very useful for managing common family business paradoxes related to HR functions, including tradition...change, merit-based...family-based, and selective...inclusive. By accepting paradoxes as special problems that cannot be "solved" but can be managed, many leaders find innovative approaches that value and tap the power of both elements of the paradox, often in mutually reinforcing ways.

Our goal here, then, is to help you take full advantage of the opportunities for both-and approaches by following a more strategic approach to HR issues, one that not only anticipates inevitable paradoxes in a number of areas but embraces them and creates value from them for the business and the family. The idea of paradox will be an ongoing theme in this book, with related content in multiple chapters. It is important to emphasize here that there is not one single answer to each paradoxical issue, but the ideas in this book will help each business family find the solution that works best for them.

Who Can Benefit from This Book

As emphasized earlier, HR can be considered everyone's responsibility within the family business. So most anyone working for or with the business can benefit from the approaches in this book. But we wrote it with several specific audience groups in mind.

- *HR professionals in family business.* This is the most obvious group that will benefit from the ideas here, as dealing with HR issues is included in their titles and job descriptions. Our goal for this group is to encourage them to take a more holistic, strategic approach to a range of issues in the family business, which means taking on the role of strategic partner rather than administrator. This approach includes developing a deeper understanding of the issues and dynamics of family business—as many HR professionals in family business do not have formal training or experience in this regard—and utilizing that understanding to develop and implement more effective HR systems, processes, and policies.

- *Family business owners, executives, and other managers (non-HR) in family business.* As we said earlier, many family firms have no formal HR organization, so responsibility for typical HR issues falls to the broader leadership group, across functional areas. While many of these individuals may have experience with family business, even extensive experience, they may not have thought about HR as strategically or comprehensively as they could. For this group, we want to lay out the key HR issues/areas all family firms face, and guide them in the development of effective systems and processes that fit their unique situation. Even in businesses that have a formal HR department, all management plays a key role in actually deploying HR policies and creating strong cultures. A stronger partnership between HR and ownership/management is essential to take full advantage of the potential contribution of the HR function. We want to help make that happen.

- *Advisers to family businesses.* Bankers, attorneys, accountants, consultants—family firms utilize the products and services of many different advisers to generate greater collective value. Here, too, family enterprise advisers can benefit from a better understanding of the HR issues facing family business, including optimal ways to help family members enter and exit the business, compensation approaches for family/nonfamily members, the conscious creation of high-performance cultures, and the like. This book provides perspective and practical tips on these and many other topics.

- *Boards of directors of family firms.* The board of directors of a family firm is tasked with protecting shareholder interests by overseeing and guiding the business's leadership, strategy, and tactics. Understanding the "people issues" most firms face—especially when the owning family remains deeply involved in the business—is critical to fulfilling this duty effectively.

As we will discuss at length in the "Our Model" chapter, the ideas here are relevant to a broad range of family firms—those of any shape, size, or stage. While the issues faced across firms tend to be similar, how they deal with them and the solutions they generate will depend on their individual characteristics and resources.

What Is in This Book

This book has a simple, streamlined structure to make it easy to find the content that is most relevant to you and your situation. While we recommend reading the chapters in order—because many refer to and build on topics that have been covered in previous ones—we recognize that some readers may use the book as a reference, seeking out the concepts and tips they can benefit most from *now*. Therefore, we have organized the material as follows:

- *Introduction*: The chapter you are reading now, which provides an overview of the motivation for this book, some themes that recur throughout, and an overview of its contents.
- *Our Model:* This chapter lays out our model for HR in the family business, with emphasis on how each component is related to and influences the others. We also cover several other models and frameworks in this chapter that we believe are important for understanding HR dynamics in family firms.
- *Culture:* We devote a chapter to culture because we see it as the context for all elements of HR in the family business, a context that both influences the HR components and is influenced by them.
- *Human Resource Life Cycle chapters:* Each of the chapters after culture covers one specific stage of the HR life cycle, as described earlier in this chapter:
  - Recruiting
  - Selection
  - Onboarding
  - Development
  - Exit
- *Parting Words:* In this final chapter we present some perspective on how to get started with implementing the ideas in this

book, along with several distinct topics such as how the role of HR can help in dealing with special circumstances (such as divorce) in the family business and how HR can interface with governance structures within a family firm such as the family council and board of directors.

Each chapter includes multiple examples of family business HR issues, along with frameworks for approaching these, visual depictions of key concepts, practical tools you can use, insightful tips, and call-out boxes to emphasize specific points and ideas. Many of the examples represent composites of firms that we know, rather than the circumstances and actions of specific firms. In cases in which we use examples and insights from identifiable firms, we have either drawn on material in the public domain or obtained permission to use the example from the businesses in question.

It Is about Constant Evolution—and One Size Will Not Fit All

We are excited to start this conversation with you about how to create a strategic, high-value role for HR within your business. We also want to emphasize that this book is just that: a start to an ongoing conversation, rather than a self-contained, one-way "lecture" with a clear endpoint. As you will see in the subsequent chapters, we emphasize repeatedly the idea of *constant evolution*, or the notion that your approach to HR will change over time, as your situation, knowledge, and goals shift. So it is about learning to use ideas, principles, and insights to drive ongoing growth. It is more about the journey than the destination; in fact, there's no single destination, but a set of targets that change over time with your business and the people within it. That is the idea of constant evolution, and we encourage you to embrace it in the way that is best for your unique situation.

In fact, keep in mind throughout this book that a one-size-fits-all approach *will not* work. We are presenting principles that can be applied to your HR thinking, processes, and systems in a way that makes the most sense for your business and family. So aim to learn the core ideas here, and then use them to create the most appropriate solutions for your situation.

Things to Remember

At the end of each chapter we will present an at-a-glance summary of the main ideas from the chapter. Here are the main things to remember from this introductory chapter:

- Our aim with this book is to help you create optimal HR systems and practices for the long-term success of your family business.
- We define "HR" as not only the function, role, and processes typically associated with the term, but also the broad set of activities involved in the HR life cycle within a company: recruiting, selection, onboarding, development, and exit.
- We see all managers within a business as playing a role in HR, so the ideas in this book apply to any manager.
- HR is a critical function in any company but especially in a family firm, as family businesses tend to treat all employees as family, must deal sensitively with managing both family and nonfamily employees, and often have longtime reputations and special cultures to treasure and preserve. How family firms manage HR strategically has helped them outperform nonfamily firms on key financial and less tangible measures. Treating HR as a strategic partner is important to continuing and strengthening this trend.
- Family businesses face many paradoxical "either-or" issues such as "family or business," and are well served to transform these into "both-ands" by finding creative ways to balance the needs and interests of different perspectives in the family and the business.
- A wide range of audiences can benefit from the ideas in this book, including family business HR professionals, family business owners/executives, family business advisers, and the boards of directors of family firms.
- We emphasize the need to aim for "constant evolution" with regard to your HR systems and practices, learning as you grow, trying new things, and recognizing that a one-size-fits-all approach rarely works in a family firm.

2

Our Model

This chapter focuses squarely on the bigger picture, with the intent of providing you a stronger foundation on which to build a plan for improving your HR policies, practices, and structures.

We have titled this chapter "Our Model," but in reality, it covers *multiple* frameworks and ideas, all related to understanding and addressing HR issues within the family business. First we consider the *evolution* of HR within a family firm, or how the size, stage, and complexity of your business may shape how you think about HR issues. This entails a review of the typical evolution of the HR function in a family firm context. Next, we present the idea of *parallel planning*, that is, how it is important to think about the business *and* the family simultaneously on several important dimensions, which provides a platform that informs HR decisions and practices.[1] After setting that important context, we talk about *our model*, which proposes that the HR life cycle components—recruiting, selection, and so on—are linked to one another dynamically and influence one another in a bidirectional manner, thus shaping the broader culture in which they exist (it will all make sense, we promise!). Finally, we review the well-established *3-Circle Framework* for family business, which outlines the three main overlapping systems involved in family business—family, ownership, and business—and how they intersect and interact in areas of importance to HR.

The Evolution of HR within a Family Firm

While the model we developed applies generally to firms of all shapes, sizes, generations, and sectors, we recognize that these variables will influence how you may employ our ideas and advice. The need to consciously manage the HR life cycle through well-considered HR practices exists in smaller, simpler family firms as well as in larger, more complex family enterprises. HR evolves over time as a business grows and advances. In the early stages, the complex, diverse aspects of the HR life cycle are taken care of by the founders and their business partners as they work tirelessly to build the business. As family firms progress, they may hire a single HR administrator who focuses on the transactional aspects of HR (e.g., payroll, benefits) and may provide some recruiting support as well. As family businesses expand to 50+ employees and beyond, a growing need for standard HR systems and structures emerges. At this stage, the HR role is still primarily transactional, but may support additional aspects of the HR life cycle (e.g., selection, development, and the like). Over time, HR will increase in size, complexity, and service offerings with the growth of the business, and it will also strengthen its position as a strategic partner at the senior levels of the company (see Figure 2.1).

In larger businesses—but especially family businesses—the HR life cycle needs to be supported by HR specialists who bring consistency and alignment across the organization to HR systems and processes. It is important to note that, although the HR function provides

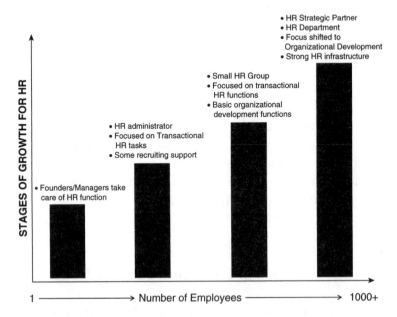

Figure 2.1   Stages of growth for the HR role in family business.

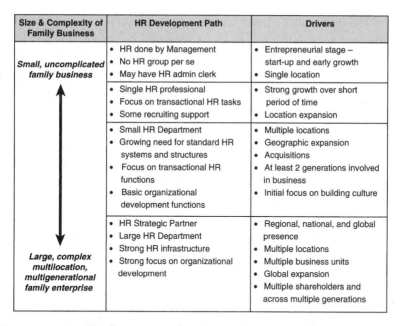

Size & Complexity of Family Business	HR Development Path	Drivers
Small, uncomplicated family business	• HR done by Management • No HR group per se • May have HR admin clerk	• Entrepreneurial stage – start-up and early growth • Single location
	• Single HR professional • Focus on transactional HR tasks • Some recruiting support	• Strong growth over short period of time • Location expansion
	• Small HR Department • Growing need for standard HR systems and structures • Focus on transactional HR functions • Basic organizational development functions	• Multiple locations • Geographic expansion • Acquisitions • At least 2 generations involved in business • Initial focus on building culture
Large, complex multilocation, multigenerational family enterprise	• HR Strategic Partner • Large HR Department • Strong HR infrastructure • Strong focus on organizational development	• Regional, national, and global presence • Multiple locations • Multiple business units • Global expansion • Multiple shareholders and across multiple generations

Figure 2.2   Drivers for HR growth and complexity.

significant guidance and support for line management, immediate responsibility for the departmental HR life cycle will always rest with the operational manager. As we indicated in the introduction, HR specialists are put in place to support managers in the design and execution of the life cycle with the goal of attracting, developing, and retaining high-performing employees.

Figure 2.1 offers a conceptual model for understanding the stages of development in the HR function over time, which will vary from family firm to family firm. This is not a prescriptive model, but instead provides a framework for anticipating expected stages of growth in the HR function. Figure 2.2 further expands on this notion by identifying a set of drivers for HR's growth and complexity.

Parallel Planning

Now that we have a better shared understanding of the HR function in family businesses, we can turn to the idea of parallel planning for the business and the family. Many family businesses tend to focus on planning for *either* the family *or* the business, and it is rare to find firms that plan comprehensively for *both* systems. The reality is that erring on either extreme will be detrimental to both components. A business that fails to create a business plan with clear guiding values and vision for its operations, along with a strategy addressing current market challenges, will most likely fail. Similarly, a family that fails to articulate its values, culture, and voice with a plan for what it is hoping to create together as a family will be unable to provide strong guidance and support to its business. As discussed in the introduction, it is not business *or* family, but business *and* family. The parallel planning process is key to making that desired balance a reality.

The "both-and" approach described in the introduction means both business and family needs must be taken into account when planning for the present and future. This concept of "parallel planning" was first proposed by our colleagues Randel Carlock and John L. Ward.[2] The overarching purpose of the parallel planning model is

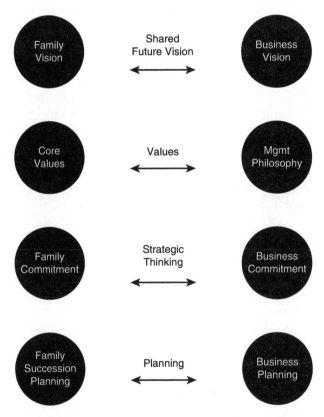

Figure 2.3   Parallel planning process.

to ensure the business strategy is aligned with and supports the family's interests (see Figure 2.3). We review it here because it provides a strong foundation on which to develop your firm's HR practices. The interplay of business and family planning requires attention to critical HR issues. For example, does it make sense to actively seek family employees? What is the best process for helping family members transition to business roles? How do we set and manage expectations for family members' performance in the business? The parallel planning model helps family businesses gain clarity on their vision, values, and strategy, which then shapes the desired culture and guides HR practices.

Let us consider the four dimensions of parallel planning, along with important questions to ask within each, as a prelude to working on your HR system and practices.[3]

- *Shared future vision.* A shared, sustainable vision of the future guides the family and the business, balancing the needs of each, along with elaborating on how family ownership can be a strategic advantage.
- *Values.* This dimension can be seen as the foundation of parallel planning, as it involves the family's shared beliefs and values, which in turn inform the business's values, philosophy, culture, and vision.
- *Strategic thinking.* The family's expectations, capabilities, values, and needs can serve as a filter and means of alignment for the business strategy. Both the business and the family can plan strategically for growth (in terms of financials and number of family members), keeping the elements above in mind.
- *Planning.* This is the realization or "operationalization" of the previous items, or how the family and business will turn values, strategy, and vision into measurable results for all stakeholders over the long term—using talent, systems, plans, practices, and metrics.

Table 2.1 presents a sample set of key questions to ask for each of the parallel planning dimensions. Some are more general questions, and others speak directly to HR issues.

Subsequent chapters go into much greater depth on the process of "operationalizing"—how to turn values, visions, and strategy into results using talent, systems, structure, and practices, especially in

Table 2.1 Questions for each planning dimension

Family	Dimension	Business
• Do we want to be a multigenerational family enterprise? Why or why not? • How can we support the business's vision with our family's capabilities and other resources?	*Shared Future Vision*	• What is our vision for the business? • What will it take to achieve our vision, especially with regard to HR factors?
• What are our core family values? • Why is the family choosing to own this particular business? • Why are we in business together?	*Values*	• What is the purpose for the business? • On what values do we want to build/expand the business?
• What are the family's goals, in terms of risk and liquidity? • How does the talent we have in the family support (or not support) our envisioned strategy?	*Strategic Thinking*	• What is the right strategy for the business, given our family values and capability, vision, market situation, culture, and values? • What is the right set of HR practices to implement the strategy?
• *Resources:* What resources does the family have—good communication, patient capital, leadership, governance, and the like—to support the business? • *Roles:* What roles do family members want or hope for in the business (or its governance) now and longer term? Are members suited to their desired roles? • *Responsibilities:* What business responsibilities are family members suited to and interested in? • *Feedback:* How will family members get constructive feedback on their performance?	*Planning*	• *Resources:* What resources does the business need to support its strategy and vision? • *Structure:* What is the best structure for the business, given our vision and strategy? How/where will family talent fit in this structure? • *Roles:* Do we have a preference for family or nonfamily employees or a combination? If we have similarly qualified candidates, do we select family over nonfamily? Why or why not? • *Responsibilities:* What responsibilities are best suited to family employees, given their talents and interests?

the HR domain. Let us consider that imperative in the context of our model of HR in the family business.

Our Model of HR in Family Business

Our experience dealing with complex HR issues in a range of family businesses has resulted in a dynamic, multilayered model of HR in family firms, as depicted in Figure 2.4. As you can see, the model consists of three different levels, each of which is related to the others:

- Family values, vision, and purpose
- Culture
- HR life cycle: recruiting, selection, onboarding, development, and exit

As the model suggests, parallel planning for the business and family drives the vision, values, and purpose, which in turn influence the culture. Culture, though not a specific stage or phase of the HR life cycle, influences every stage of that cycle and, really, everything that happens in the firm, which will be discussed at length in the chapter

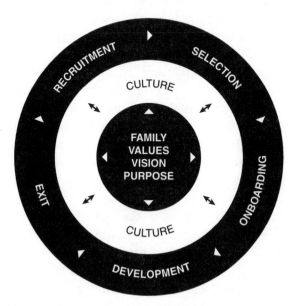

Figure 2.4   Our model of HR in family business.

on culture. As a brief summary, we view culture as the shared values and beliefs, practices, policies, and means by which your firm represents itself internally and externally. We advocate strongly for building culture "*consciously*" by being explicit about *where* your culture comes from (typically from the family's values, as mentioned above), *what* you would like your culture to be, and *how* to build and monitor the culture that is right for your firm.

Culture, in turn, influences, supports, and is influenced by the *HR life cycle*, the outermost level of our model, represented by the following stages (each with a summary of our approach to it):

- *Recruiting:* Recruiting is about where to find the right people to hire as employees. We suggest a *"reverse-funnel" approach* to hiring: rather than considering the universe of all possible employees, it is more effective and efficient to do significant upfront thinking to understand which types of candidates are the right ones for your family firm—by asking key questions about what is best for the business and family—and then using the answers and themes that emerge to identify potential candidates from within and outside the family.

- *Selection:* Selection is the natural step after recruiting, which involves choosing the best candidates to hire from the small pool of candidates you have considered more seriously. Many family businesses approach selection in a casual, informal manner. However, we recommend a *systematic* approach to selection, to ensure choosing the best candidates, which has multiple important implications for the business and, in turn, the family. Components of a systematic approach to selection include clarity on the job description/terms, a range of means to assess candidate fit, a clear process for making hiring decisions and negotiating terms of hire, and a planned process for introducing new hires—especially family employees—to the firm.

- *Onboarding:* Onboarding is the specific way in which you bring new hires into the firm. Formerly known narrowly as "orientation," onboarding is better conceived as an important form of *integration*, a longer-term program and process that brings employees seamlessly into the firm through enhanced understanding of the business/family history, values, and culture; their roles/responsibilities; and the development of early, important knowledge and relationships. The optimal approach to onboarding takes a long-term view of the process as unfolding over months rather than days, and is built on the idea that the arrival of new employees means a *two-way adjustment*, for both the business and the new hires.

- *Development:* Development is the means by which you grow the capabilities of your people, aligned with the strategy, vision, culture, and needs of the firm. As we see it, an ideal development system reflects a *continuous process of learning and growth.* More specifically, we conceive of development as a cycle with the components of performance evaluation and gap analysis; outcomes (both positive *and* negative) and development planning; learning; and coaching, with the last two components as a "cycle within a cycle." Taking people through this iterative cycle boosts their competence, interpersonal and leadership capabilities, contributions, and engagement with the firm.

- *Exit:* Exit is just that, the means by which people depart from the business. We see exit not as a time-limited event but a *transition* involving multiple types of reorientation for all parties. The transition an exit represents is ideally a deliberate, careful process, with consideration of the type of exit (voluntary or involuntary) and a systematic approach to the periods leading up to, during, and after the actual departure. Taking care with exits ensures the departing employee and the business derive value from the process, while avoiding potential risks and damage associated with this highly sensitive transition.

We want to emphasize the multidirectional, dynamic nature of our model. Each component is influenced by, and then, in turn, influences the others. As an example, selection will be influenced by a firm's culture, as the culture will guide the choice of new hires based on perceived values and other factors. At the same time, the way new hires, especially in management roles, carry out their responsibilities and interact with colleagues powerfully influences the culture, or at the very least its expression. Consider a scenario we have observed: a family-owned financial services firm in the southern United States was helmed by its founder until he was ready to retire in his mid-70s. The company hired its first nonfamily CEO because he appeared to be a strong cultural fit with the firm (based on the founder's values)—he was a hard worker with deep commitment to results. But as the new CEO's tenure lengthened, his emphasis on operations, policy, and risk management—he was a former attorney—began to shift the culture to become more about risk management, standardization, and documentation rather than relationships—internally and externally—and trust. Ultimately, he and the company decided to part ways, as his approach was misaligned with the firm's deeper values and culture. His exit again shifted the cultural features, but this time to their original "settings."

This example illustrates how the different levels and components of our model interact with and influence one another, promoting both positive evolution and less favorable adaptation or change. Like some cell walls, each component of the model is permeable, ideally allowing nutrients in while flushing waste out. Importantly, the dynamic nature of our model reflects the constant evolution any firm undergoes. The system—including all components in our model—may be in an ongoing state of flux, and the right approach can help orient the evolution toward growth rather than chaos.

The 3-Circle Model

One final framework that is important and significant to HR in a family business is the 3-Circle model for understanding complexities in family enterprise. All family businesses consist of three overlapping systems: family, business, and ownership, as suggested by Figure 2.5.[4] A system, as we use it in this context, is any organized

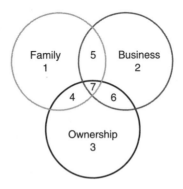

Figure 2.5 The 3-Circle framework for family business.

and interacting collection of people, structures, and processes that forms a complex whole, and where that whole is greater than the simple summation of its parts. In the case of the 3-Circle framework specifically, the family system is that group of people—along with their supporting structures and processes—who are related to one another (through blood, marriage, adoption, etc.). The business system, by comparison, contains those who work in the family enterprise on a regular basis. Finally, the ownership system is made up of those individuals who have equity in the family's business. This deceptively simple model is important to understand for anyone working with HR within a family firm for several reasons.

First, it is important to note that each system has a different purpose and that these purposes can sometimes be contrasting and conflicting on multiple levels. The primary purpose of the family system is nurturing and developing members' self-esteem as well as sharing common values. Each family operates with its own style, role relationships, rules, and ways of dealing with conflict and expressing emotions. The family system is a very private and personal space. In contrast, a business system is concerned with operational effectiveness and making a profit. It is a public space in which we have our social controls in place. It is a more objective and, theoretically, adaptive environment than the family system. Finally, the ownership system is focused on the viability of the enterprise and return on investment. The lines that distinguish one system from another can easily become blurred, and awareness of these different systems is essential for managing them effectively.

Second, people occupy different roles in the framework, which often creates tension and anxiety within the system as a whole. As the numbers in the figure suggest, there are seven unique positions an individual might occupy, each with a different perspective, set of interests, and concerns. Some people will be members of all three circles (such as the founder/CEO—position 7), while others may fall into two systems (such as a family member who owns shares but is employed outside the business—position 4) or just one system (such as a nonfamily manager with no equity—position 2). The roles for any given individual can change over time, adding another layer of complexity. Awareness and management of these different positions and perspectives is critical for dealing with any kind of HR issue.

Third, in the context of systems thinking, it is important for those dealing with HR issues to understand how the three parts of the family business system (family, business, and ownership) *intersect and interact, at the system and the individual level.* So when one part of the system changes, it has a reverberating impact on the other two systems. The three key principles of systems thinking are listed next.[5]

1. *Every action has a reaction*—and these reactions may be disproportionate to the action (a small issue in one circle can have a big impact in another).
2. *Families seek homeostasis*—so when one part of the system changes, the rest of the system works hard to maintain the status quo (even if the status quo is not constructive).
3. *Patterns of behavior repeat themselves* over generations—these patterns can be vast and varied in their nature, including those related to behavioral (e.g., communication styles), physical (e.g., health issues, addictions), functional (e.g., education, career choices), and other areas.

It is helpful for HR to see the whole system (and not just the business part), so that they can assist families in managing and mitigating the impact of change from the business circle on the rest of the system.

For example, HR specialists can be instrumental in helping families establish boundaries (not barriers) between the family and the business, such as when and where it is appropriate for family shareholders outside the family enterprise to voice their concerns about business strategy or operations.

Now let us consider how interaction among the circles occurs at the system—rather than individual—level, or how collective issues in one circle affect the other two circles. As depicted in Figure 2.6, many paths of influence start with the family circle. The family's vision and values, for example, will affect both the ownership goals and the business's vision and strategy.

A family with a vision of high-impact philanthropy, for example, will want to generate profits to invest in the community, which will require a specific vision or growth strategy for the business to fund the charitable activities. Similarly, large-scale changes in the business—the simplest example is a major swing in profitability, or even the threat of folding—will inevitably affect the owning family, as

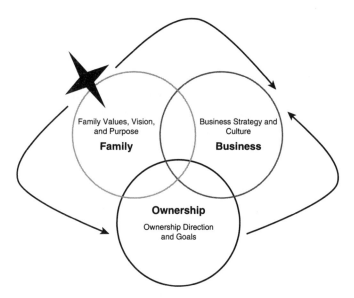

Figure 2.6   Interaction among the 3 Circles of family business.

their livelihood and assets are often tied up in the business, and their lifestyle is directly dependent on its profitability.

Now let us consider the individual level within the 3-Circle framework, where there will again be dynamic influence and interaction among the parts. Individuals occupy different positions in the three circles, which may create tension within and between individuals, including as related to HR. For example, someone who is in position 4 (see Figure 2.5) in the three circles—family owner—may expect to enter the third circle (business) more easily than others (i.e., family nonowners) might, and this may be a true or false assumption, depending on the values and culture of the family enterprise as a whole. In addition, some family owners may feel that they are not given adequate information about the business because they are not part of the business system, or "insiders." Such individuals may feel they are treated as secondary because of their role and place in the overall system. As such, a good practice is to ensure that *all* owners are informed, educated, and valued as part of the overall system. They need and deserve accurate information, good leadership/management, and profitability.

There is no formula that can determine exactly how the circles that make up your family business will interact. It will depend on many factors, including the values, culture, situation, and people involved. The most important contribution of this framework is to provide a big-picture view illustrating that what happens in one circle will most likely affect the others, sometimes in subtle, hard-to-detect ways. Those working on HR issues, for example, will be served well by stepping outside the business circle to understand the impact of these issues, at any stage of the life cycle, have on the other domains. In short, almost nothing happens in isolation, and the HR function can focus its efforts more successfully when this context is understood and applied appropriately.

Because little happens in isolation, there are many circumstances in which it will be of benefit to actively manage the impact an event or interaction will have in the other parts of the system. At one family business we know, three second-generation siblings—two sisters and a brother—worked together, each contributing ideas and initiatives to the firm. When the younger sister returned to work after business school, she argued to implement several major strategy and operations-related change initiatives. The brother, who held a higher-level role in the business, disagreed, and the father (founder and CEO) sided with him. As tensions rose, their mother (the founder's wife), who did not hold an official role in the business, became involved, urging the father and brother to reconsider. The other sister avoided the situation entirely. Sunday night family dinners, once events that were much looked forward to, became fraught with tension, and soon one or more of the siblings avoided the meal altogether. When the younger daughter said she was considering leaving the firm, her father countered that only second-generation members employed by the business could earn/retain ownership—a policy he developed mostly in reaction to the situation. Business-related tensions had bled quickly into the family and ownership circles.

This example illustrates starkly the importance of understanding the interaction of the three circles, and that families and HR need to work together to understand how to establish boundaries and good practices such as family participation policies, effective governance, decision-making, and communication structures. The family noted above was ultimately able to do that with outside help.

A good understanding of the 3-Circle framework and its dynamics is critical for approaching HR issues as strategically as possible. Remember: nothing happens in isolation.

Things to Remember

In this chapter we have presented several big-picture ideas, models, and frameworks for understanding HR in family business. Here are the main things to remember.

- *Firm size and complexity* will influence HR issues. The ideas in this book are relevant to family firms of all shapes, sizes, and generational stages. But the firm's size and level of complexity will influence the nature of the roles and processes involved in HR—from no formal HR group to a large HR department. In any scenario, the HR function is best seen as a strategic component of any business.
- *Parallel planning* is at the core of our HR model, such that the family firm needs to attend to long-term thinking related to both the business and family, including on the dimensions of values, strategic thinking, shared future vision, and formulation of plans. The output of parallel planning establishes the vision, values, and strategy of the business and, in turn, the culture and HR processes we will discuss.
- *Our model* of HR in family business places the family vision, values, purpose at the core, with subsequent layers including culture and the HR life cycle components: recruiting, selection, onboarding, development, and exit. Each layer has a bidirectional influence on the others, as part of a dynamic, interactive model. Each of the following chapters in the book will discuss in greater detail one of the stages of the life cycle.
- *The 3-Circle framework* is a well-established model of family business that considers how three systems—family, business, and ownership—interact in any family firm. It is important to note that the framework results in seven unique positions that any given individual can have within the system, each with its own perspective and interests. Interaction occurs among the three systems (collectively) and the individuals within them, and it is important to understand this when dealing with any HR issue—within a family business, nothing happens in isolation.

3

Culture

At the heart of Kal Tire is a culture steeped in values. Seven guiding principles known as the Aims were developed to provide a road map for the 5,000+ team members. These Aims are meant to be used as a guide for how business will be conducted and provide team members a foundation from which to work and make decisions. They are principles to always strive for, not goals to complete.[1]

That is the introduction to the "Aims" page of the website of Kal Tire, a Canadian tire sales and service company with 5,500 team members running over 250 stores and 170 mine sites worldwide that generate $1.5 billion (CDN) in annual revenues, making it Canada's largest independent tire dealer. Kal Tire's seven Aims—such as "Our aim is to conduct ourselves with honesty and integrity, being conscious of our image and with modest respect for our successes" (the full list appears later in the chapter)—help guide team member behavior related to customers, suppliers, and one another. "The Aims represent how we like to see ourselves when we're at our best," said Ken Chaun, Senior VP Retail Group. "By looking at the Aims we can understand how to react to most situations."

The Aims also reflect the values of the family behind Kal Tire. "The company is professionally managed, but still very much of a family business," Chaun said. Tom and Norah Foord started the business in 1953 in the small town of Vernon, British Columbia. Kal Tire's values-based culture reflects their sense of identity—including an emphasis on modesty and service—as well as Vernon's low-key culture. "Our parking lot doesn't have a lot of fancy automobiles," Chaun said. "Norah never bought a new car, and even our president [a second-generation family member] drives a 16-year-old car."

Despite its strength, Kal Tire's culture was not always so conscious. The idea to formalize the Aims arose in the 1990s, when the company acquired a competitor, doubling in size overnight. With a much larger, more far-flung team, the family and other leaders believed it was important to explain "who they are and how they do things." After developing the Aims, Kal Tire placed them on posters in every office and meeting room, as a strong visual reminder of the firm's value and culture. "Even today we still spend a lot of time talking about the Aims and what they mean to us," Chaun said. The HR department takes direction from the Aims in all aspects of its interaction with employees.

Kal Tire's approach to culture has been a clear driver of the company's success.

*   *   *

Kal Tire's Aims and how its employees live by them are a great example of developing a strong conscious culture, one that can be a core asset for a family business. While your firm's culture can help boost performance, morale, and other success factors, it is a dynamic, evolving business feature that can also become a barrier to the achievement of strategic objectives. In order to maximize its positive contribution, culture must be understood and approached in a conscious way. In fact, there is a growing appreciation for the importance and power of culture, summed up in the popular phrase attributed to business guru Peter Drucker: "Culture eats strategy for breakfast."[2] Strategy, while crucial to business success, is supported (or hindered) by an organization's underlying culture, which can be harder to identify, understand, and shape. Culture, then, is foundational to your family and business—it underlies everything.

We believe that family values inform business culture both directly (as represented within the firm's internal environment and practices) and indirectly (through the board's influence, for example, which typically reflects the family's values), as depicted in Figure 3.1. In this context, what is your firm's (and family's) culture? Is it the right culture for your family's business? If not, how can you make it so? (And, of course, what's right for your business today may not be the best fit down the road.) Kal Tire and many other family firms routinely face culture-related questions, sometimes without even recognizing

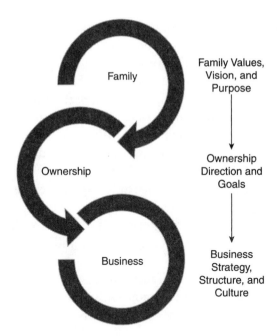

Figure 3.1   How family values inform business culture.

them. While the idea that culture is important is not new, getting your arms around it and cultivating your desired culture can be challenging. To help you address these issues in a practical way, in this chapter we dive deep into culture-related issues in a family business, especially as it relates to HR.

To make the link between culture and HR in a family firm, we first have to talk about business culture in general. Some firms, family and nonfamily, make culture *explicit*, labeling it "The _____ Way," with the firm's (or family's) name in the blank, and providing lists of do's and don'ts related to values and behavior. Kal Tire's seven Aims are a great example of this.

1. Our aim is to earn the trust of our customers by providing them with a level of quality and value of both service and products that exceeds their expectations and exceeds that available from the competition.
2. Our aim is that the career of every team member is supported by quality leadership, training, and opportunities for advancement. Our people will work safely and have the ambition,

enthusiasm, and energy to be productive, efficient, and contribute to an upbeat atmosphere in the workplace.

3. Our aim is to achieve a fair profit in all of our operations.

4. Our aim is to expand our company in a deliberate and balanced fashion for the purpose of strengthening our ability to serve the customer and provide a solid future for our people. However, our rate of expansion will not be beyond our ability to finance or manage to a consistent standard of quality.

5. Our aim is to conduct ourselves with honesty and integrity, being conscious of our image and with modest respect for our successes. Our image is defined by the conduct of each of us.

6. Our aim is to build long-term relationships with our suppliers based on competitiveness, value, and mutual respect of objectives.

7. Our aim is to continually improve every aspect of our company, recognizing our responsibility to our customers, each other, our communities, and the environment.

Other firms take a more *implicit* approach, with their culture evident in the way they treat employees, customers, suppliers, and other stakeholders—as guided by unspoken rules within the organization. Both can be effective means of conveying culture. A succinct way of looking at culture is as both the determinant and reflection of what you say, do, feel, believe, value, and measure in your organization, as illustrated in Figure 3.2.

Some researchers discuss culture as made up of artifacts, perspectives, values, and assumptions.[3] More generally, you can think of culture as the "water" you swim in, or even the organizational "air" you breathe—something that is not always visible but is extremely powerful nonetheless. Culture influences everything in your business, and everything influences it. Culture is always present, even if it is unacknowledged.[4]

Thus, our definition of culture in general includes multiple mutually reinforcing elements:

- *Shared values and beliefs within the organization:* These are underlying, guiding principles regarding what the organization stands for and how it should (and does) interact with internal and external stakeholders. The beliefs can also be about

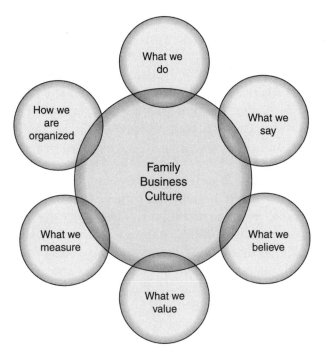

Figure 3.2   Components of family business culture.

how individuals within the firm should interact. Many firms we know uphold the core value of "respect," and expect their employees to treat one another and other stakeholders (such as customers and suppliers) with this value in mind. Note that values form the basis for most cultures, as noted above and discussed later in more detail.

- *How your firm does things, both internally and externally:* This includes the behaviors, policies, practices, and interactions at every level of the organization. Culture is at the core of your people, systems, and processes. It is about formal and informal procedures, from how the firm recruits and selects employees, to treatment of customer-service issues, to company social events. Any behavior can be seen as an expression of the firm's culture, from the way receptionists greet visitors to how executives interact with the board, but the items below represent particularly important areas.
- *How your firm represents itself:* This can be about formal representations of the firm, such as through internal symbols (like

artifacts in the lobby; one family construction firm proudly displays the founder's age-worn toolbox at the main office) or external marketing or public relations campaigns, along with the products and services the firm offers, which all have a positive or negative impact on consumers and the environment. This can also include more subtle signs, such as the company's logo or even the font (bold vs. "quieter") it uses for marketing materials.

In short, culture is a key element of any family business, whether those within the firm recognize this or not. That's a good thing for multiple reasons. First, there is significant evidence that family firms are more likely to have positive cultures than their nonfamily peers. For example, family business expert and our consulting colleague John L. Ward suggests that family companies are more likely to have positive cultures built on long-standing values, often those associated with the founding generation.[5] Such cultures, in turn, support superior business performance, continuity, and longevity.[6] Ward offers an explanation for the link: a firm's positive culture and values "both strengthen their strategy and motivate their people," leading to superior results.[7] We think a strong, positive culture is reflected in clearer direction, greater meaning for employees and other stakeholders, better coordination of action, and reduced complexity within the firm. What is more, because the cultures of family firms typically emerge from longstanding values of early generations, they can be very difficult to imitate, creating a well-protected competitive advantage. Some firms even deploy their family-based values as a *direct* way to differentiate themselves from nonfamily or other family businesses, placing these prominently on their website or marketing materials and tying them to their business value proposition.[8] Thus family firms are more likely to have positive cultures *and* benefit from them, including with regard to HR and related practices.

Accordingly, our model of HR in family business reflects a very strong emphasis on culture. Recall from our introduction chapter that the visual for our model includes culture as the factor surrounding all HR-related processes. As suggested above, culture informs *every* process within the firm, and is crucial for HR, as employees' actions both are shaped by firm culture and at the same time shape (create) that culture: culture is action, and action is culture. You can think of culture as the glue keeping all parts of the organization together and aligned. That means having the right culture for your business and situation can lead to more "stickiness" among the components.

But cultivating the right culture for your firm is no easy task. In fact, many family firms overlook the importance of culture, or the role of HR within it. This chapter explores the sources and effects of culture, the importance of a "conscious culture" with regard to HR, and ways of developing, promoting, and monitoring the right culture for your firm, as well as culture-related pitfalls.

A Conscious Culture Is Paramount

One of us comes from a family-owned manufacturing business that had two separate operating locations. In one of the facilities, employees bought their coffee from a vending machine in the breakroom, while in the other, employees contributed to a "coffee fund" and took turns brewing coffee daily for everyone in the facility. This simplest of differences illustrates a larger-scale contrast in cultures between the facilities: one emphasized autonomy, whereas the other was more about pooling resources and sharing knowledge. It was not clear exactly how the culture of each facility had evolved, or whether employees recognized the difference. But it was there, evident in the way people worked together—or did not—in each facility. This chapter is about how to take a more "conscious" approach to culture within your firm.

Let us consider how culture originates, and then dive more deeply into the concept of a conscious culture—something we recommend for every family business.

Origins of Culture

Like any superhero, culture in a family business should have a good story about its origin. How does culture typically come about? As suggested above and exemplified by Kal Tire, it is usually rooted firmly in a business's values—in a family business, these are almost always the family's values, as originated by the founding generation and influenced by factors including history and religion. As

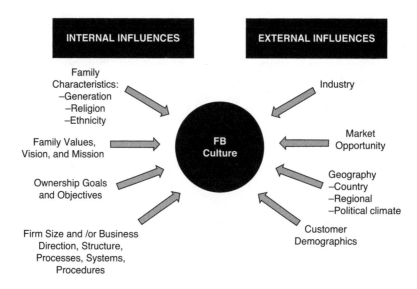

Figure 3.3 Factors shaping a firm's culture.

Figure 3.3 suggests, the family's values form the roots of culture, but these are lived and shaped specifically by each successive generation of owners. So we can think of culture as both driven by values and as a means of expressing these values internally and externally.

Note, however, that some business families set out to build a culture that is expressive of their values and fall short. Others think their culture expresses a certain set of values, but in reality it does not. In later sections, we will discuss how to move toward the best-fitting culture for your firm. The "Historical Influences on Family Values" worksheet is helpful in articulating how a family's history as well as other historical events have influenced the family and its values. Table 3.1 shows how family values inform business culture.

Culture may also be shaped by factors internal or external to the family/firm, whether through an influence on the family's values or not. Such factors include the following:

- *Market opportunity:* Culture will be influenced by a business's "opportunity environment." That is, an opportunity-rich environment such as a high-growth market may breed a different kind of culture (often one marked by dynamism and high energy) than an environment with fewer routes to growth. But culture can also be independent of this influence. We have all seen companies with highly dynamic cultures in even the most mature industries.

Table 3.1 Historical influences on family values worksheet

Timeline	Identify Your Family's History and Other Historical Events	Reflect on How This Influenced Your Family's Values
Early Family History– 1800s		
Traditionalists (1900–1944)		
Baby Boomers (1945–1964)		
Generation X (1965–1980)		
Generation Y (1981–1999)		
Generation Z (including Millennials) (2000-today)		

- *Industry/Customer focus:* Specific industries tend to be associated with different values and cultures. The agricultural business is known for its culture of discipline and hard work. Tech start-ups are associated with fun and irreverent cultures (which do not necessarily exclude hard work!). Similarly, consumer-oriented firms may have a more people-focused culture than those in the business-to-business space, but again, this reflects a general pattern, not a hard and fast rule.
- *Geography/Ethnicity:* Of course, where a family business is located—within the world or within a specific country—will likely influence its culture, as will the dominant nationality of its owners, managers, and employees. China-based family firms, for example, are known for cultures that feature formality and hierarchy, with emphasis on deep respect for older generations. Businesses based in more rural areas may have a more traditional culture than those based in urban centers.

- *Generational stage:* The generational stage (first-, second-, third-generation, etc.) of the business ownership can influence its culture, as early and later generations often hold different values, mindsets, and approaches to business. For example, earlier generations, including founders, tend to be entrepreneurial (they started the business, after all) and paternalistic, following their gut instincts, with a strong emphasis on taking care of the family. More recent generations, in contrast, may seek to build a more professional environment with greater structure, ostensibly focusing more on the business, sometimes at the family's expense. Generational stage is correlated with size—later-generation firms tend to be larger—which also helps explain the focus on professionalization (larger firms tend to require more structure, processes and policies to coordinate action among the large employee base).

- *Generational cohort:* The generational cohort of the owners, family leaders, and employees will likely have an influence on the business's culture. Those in the United States who grew up during the economic scarcity of the Great Depression (the "Greatest" Generation) typically have a different mindset from their children (baby boomers), who were raised during a period of expansive post–World War II growth. Similarly, much has been made of the Millennial generation, including their emphasis on collaboration.[9] Entire books have been written about the interactions—especially the clashes—of different generational cohorts in a given family business, but for our purposes it is important to remember this is a factor that can affect your culture.[10]

While all of these factors can play a role in culture and some of them are less within your control, our main point is that you can and should be *intentional* about the culture you create and perpetuate. Remember: every organization has a culture, whether it is created with intention or not. The most effective organizations shape their cultures consciously. In fact, choosing *not* to become more aware of your culture or to deal actively with it will most likely result in a culture that is not ideal for your business and family on one or more dimensions.

That is why we advocate strongly developing a "conscious culture."

The Concept of a Conscious Culture

Our definition of a conscious culture is pretty simple. It is about understanding *where* your culture comes from, *what* you would like your culture to be, and *how* to build the culture that is right for your family firm and to monitor it on an ongoing basis. To break those out, think of them as

- strong awareness of your firm's *existing* culture (it is there whether you realize it or not);
- specific notions of the *ideal* culture for your organization;
- ways to make that ideal culture a *reality*; and
- ongoing *assessment* of cultural features and their impact (both positive and negative).

One key resource you will need in order to develop a conscious culture is something people often overlook: courage. You need courage to take a clear-eyed look at your business and its culture; to be able to identify gaps between where you are now and your ideal culture; and to take the conscious, deliberate steps needed to close those gaps and to keep an eye on emerging issues. For example, some firms tend to mistake rewards for respect (see the "Rewards Cannot Replace Respect" Box), and will need to take steps to shift the cultural elements that promote the desired intent.

Rewards Cannot Replace Respect

Some firms offer a very benefits-rich environment for employees, but fail to build this on basic respect for their people. While employees may appreciate large bonuses and gold-plated insurance plans, over time these benefits will come to feel like lip service if a culture of respect is missing. In our collective experience, turnover is less related to compensation and benefits, and more related to culture as expressed through the supervisory relationships. There is a reason for the popular saying "People quit their bosses, not their jobs."[11] Problems related to a low-respect culture include inferior performance (despite the higher compensation), diminished morale, and high turnover. HR researcher and consultant Marci Koblenz highlights this issue by placing respect and balance at the base of her "Work and Life Pyramid of Needs."[12]

In the next section, we discuss each key element that helps create a conscious culture in the context of your firm's HR, with the goal of offering practical tips and tools for helping you understand your current culture and move toward the culture that is right for you.

Building the Right Culture for You

Before getting into specific recommendations for approaching your culture—by assessing, formulating, acting, and monitoring—we need to make something clear: there is no one "right" culture for every firm. We are not prescribing a set of cultural components or practices that will guarantee business success and family harmony. In fact, there is no such thing. Rather, we want to help you find the right cultural fit for your firm/family. It is definitely not a one-size-fits-all issue. And before you can even think about the right culture for your firm, you have to understand the culture you currently have.

You Are Here

Have you ever stared at one of those large shopping-mall directories, looking for the route between where you are and your favorite clothing store or restaurant? It is even harder to find your way if the directory does not make clear where you currently are. In the same way, how can you move toward the right culture if you do not even know what your current culture is? You can't.

So how do you understand your current culture? First of all, informal evidence of culture is everywhere within your organization. But you have to pay attention. Do people seem enthusiastic about their work? Do they bring high levels of energy to tasks and meetings? With regard to HR, what kind of values, if any, play a role in hiring and promotion decisions? In training and development? What kind of people tend to get promoted? What kind of people are more likely to resign? The answers to these and similar questions can help you get a general sense of your firm's culture, or where it falls on the "not so great" to "pretty good" scale. Smiles, energy, and enthusiasm are much more likely near the latter. Table 3.2 shows a quick snapshot of

Table 3.2 Company cultural descriptions based on a model developed by Quinn and Cameron

Character of Culture	Clan Culture	Adhocracy Culture	Hierarchical Culture	Market Culture
Dominant characteristics	Personal and family like	Entrepreneurial and risk taking	Control and structured	Competitive and goal oriented
Leadership	Coaching, facilitative, nurturing	Innovative, higher risk tolerance, driving	Organized, coordinating, efficiency orientated	Aggressive, results focused
Management	Teamwork, consensus building, focus on participation	Independence, delegation, focus on innovation and	Planning, conformity expected, focus on predictability	Driving, task oriented, focus on achievement
Organizational glue	Loyalty and mutual trust	Commitment to innovation, development of new ideas	Formal rules and policies	Emphasis on achievement and goal accomplishment
Strategic emphasis	High trust, openness	Acquisitions of resources, creating new challenges	Permanence and stability	Competitive actions and winning
Criteria for success	Development of HR, teamwork, concern for people	Unique, new products and services	Dependable, efficient, low cost	Winning, outpacing, first to market

different firm cultural descriptions based on a model developed by Kim S. Quinn and Robert E. Cameron.[13]

There is a range of ways to measure culture: from quick to time consuming, from free to expensive, from simple to complex, and from off-the-shelf to highly customized. So it is important to think about your culture-related goals and the resources you want to expend on these. Below are the main categories of culture assessment tools.

Satisfaction/"pulse" surveys: Simple employee satisfaction/engagement surveys may not help you identify the specific nature of your culture, but the results will probably help you understand whether your firm has culture-related issues. Unhappy, disengaged people are usually part of a suboptimal and/or ill-fitting culture. As more family firms understand the value of simple surveys and polls, such instruments have become even more common on the business landscape, with some firms even measuring engagement and other variables through weekly "pulse surveys."[14] These kinds of fast and cheap tools offer general measures of culture that can be important starting points.

Group exercises: Several types of exercises can help you understand features of your current culture. We use a Family Values Exercise that can be completed by family, employees, and other key stakeholders (Board members, customers, suppliers, and others), as outlined in Table 3.3. It asks participants to describe the values they see the company living on a regular basis. If the company culture is strong, then the values observed by others will closely match the core values espoused by the business/family. Regardless of the match, such an exercise can yield valuable insights on your current culture.

Another way of getting at firm values is by first looking at individual values, as measured by exercises such as card sorts. Dennis T. Jaffe and Cynthia D. Scott developed a card sort that allows individuals to prioritize their top values—with categories including mastery, inner development, and relationships, as well as others—and then using their rankings to help decide what collective values matter most.[15] While values are important foundations of culture, it is important to focus on a smaller set that matter most to you, as recent research suggests (see "The Rule of No More Than Four" Box).

Table 3.3   Family values exercise

List of Values:

Achievement	*Honesty*
Adaptability	*Humor*
Aggressiveness	*Independence*
Authority	*Innovation*
Autonomy	*Knowledge*
Caring	*Merit*
Caution	*Nature*
Challenge	*Obedience*
Change	*Peace*
Community	*Perseverance*
Competition	*Power*
Consensus	*Principled*
Courage	*Professionalism*
Creativity	*Prosperity*
Democracy	*Quality*
Diplomacy	*Rationality*
Equality	*Recognition*
Experimentation	*Respect*
Fairness	*Security*
Family	*Self-control*
Forgiveness	*Stability*
Friendship	*Teamwork*
Fun	*Tolerance*
Hard work	*Tradition*
Harmony	*Transparency*

Note: We ask family members to review a list of 50 values and identify the 10 that best define their family today (they can add additional values to the list as needed). After they choose their top 10, they are asked to choose 5 that should be a priority for the family, and to share both lists (top 10 and top 5) with other family members, looking for themes/patterns/surprises. The family can also discuss whether they want to identify specific aspirational values for the future.

The Rule of No More Than Four

Recent research from the Wharton School of Business suggests that leaders can help create a stronger sense of shared purpose in their organizations by communicating a small number of values by using rich visual imagery.[16] The researchers studied hospitals specifically, and found that this combination of values and visuals boosted performance by triggering a stronger sense of the ultimate goal and better coordination among employees. They also found that leaders tended to communicate visions without imagery and discuss too many values, prompting the recommendation that organizations identify no more than four values and use significant visual imagery to convey values and vision.

Culture-specific surveys: Multiple surveys have been developed to assess corporate culture. One longstanding research-based example is based on the Denison Organizational Model, and involves gathering information from management on their perception of the business's culture.[17] The data collected are then used to place the firm's culture on a two-dimensional model involving focus (internal vs. external) and stability (stable vs. flexible). Similarly, a simple survey developed by John L. Ward places family business cultures on a spectrum from "family-first" to "business-first," reflecting which of the two the business tends to emphasize more, as suggested by members' survey responses.[18]

Third-party assessments: Several consulting firms offer organizational culture/behavior assessments. For example, Human Synergistics, based in the US Midwest, conducts an Organizational Culture Inventory to help characterize a firm's culture on key dimensions related broadly to dimensions of constructiveness or defensiveness (the former drives better performance).[19] The consultancy also offers a special version of the inventory to assess what leaders and employees view as an ideal culture for the organization. Similarly, Polarity Partnerships (Dr. Barry Johnson, Founder) offers a customizable tool and consulting services to help family businesses understand the key polarities with which they are struggling as an organization, along with steps to address related issues.[20] Such measures can be the most time consuming and expensive, but they may also yield the most specific, objective results and implications.

Regardless of the approach chosen, the HR function can lead the process, with management not only supporting the value of it, vocally, but also committing to doing something meaningful with the results. HR is well positioned to help connect the dots between the expressed values of the owning family and the culture of the business.

Where You Want To Be

Once you are more aware of your current culture, you can think about how to move toward a more ideal culture for your organization at this time. Like we said previously, there is no single ideal culture for all firms. The right fit will depend on many of the factors we talked about before, including your industry, geography, and generation. But one factor stands out above the others: your values. Values are the most powerful force in shaping organizational and familial cultures. In our experience, the better-performing—and happiest— family businesses tend to have strong cultures shaped by explicitly stated and agreed-upon values. These often originate with the founding generation, and are then translated and modified to reflect subsequent generations and business situations. So our advice in this section is anchored by the idea of creating a values-driven culture. A conscious culture for most firms is explicitly based on agreed-upon values, and the people within such cultures tend to live by these values, resulting in less ambiguity and confusion, more efficient use of resources, and superior performance and satisfaction—all part of a virtuous cycle that generates greater success. Here are some ways of identifying the right cultural fit.

Storytelling: One of the simplest ways of getting at the values you want your culture to reflect is storytelling. When family leaders are struggling with cultural issues, we often have them tell stories they have heard about the founders and/or earlier generation, ideally narratives that have been passed down among members. "What family or business stories have you heard that really stuck with you?" we ask. The resulting stories reflect, more often than not, the deeply held values of the family. For example, one business family tells the story of how the founder always invited anyone working on the house— whether a carpenter, plumber, or landscaper—to have a cup of tea with him, asking them about their lives. The simple story illustrated the founder's emphasis on community, humility, and respect, all values that the family wanted to embody in its way of doing business. So even telling the simplest stories can help you uncover and pass on the values you want to drive your culture. We like to think of this process as "appreciative inquiry." But it comes with a caveat: while family history is a fertile source of values—and, in turn, culture— that does not mean it is always best to rigidly follow these values.

Think about the situation you are in *now* and the people, family and nonfamily, involved in the business *now*, when considering what cultural elements fit best. The Family Values Exercise discussed in the previous section can also be a way of getting at the values you want the business to exemplify. Many families share these stories with management, make them part of the new employee orientation process, or even incorporate them into context-setting for strategic planning sessions.

Resolving common tensions: Another way to move toward a more effective culture for your firm is to think about polarity, specifically how to manage tensions between two seemingly opposing forces that family businesses commonly encounter. For example, all family businesses face choices between "business first" or "family first." Most family businesses naturally prefer one approach over the other, and this becomes reflected in their culture. Neither style is inherently right, as there are advantages and disadvantages associated with each. Healthy cultures find ways to value both options of a polarity, rather than pursuing one to the exclusion of the other. For example, a family that has historically emphasized results, achievement, and winning might find that their culture has evolved to become quite competitive, even to the point where internal rivalries are unproductive and distracting. By recognizing the need to value relationships along with results, management might help their culture evolve to become more collaborative, creative, and productive over time.

Thinking in categories: Academic researchers have categorized family-business cultures based on multiple frameworks. One such framework involves the assumptions held within the business along several core dimensions. Among these dimensions are the nature of relationships, beliefs about fundamental human nature, and orientation toward time (past, present, or future).[21] For example, a paternalistic culture will have more hierarchical relationships, belief patterns that see humans as less trustworthy (hence the careful oversight), and a present or past orientation. A more participative culture will be more focused on collaborative relationships, the belief that humans are basically trustworthy, and a present or future orientation. A different framework categorizes culture along dimensions of stability and focus, as mentioned above.[22] In this scheme, a "hierarchy" culture is more focused on stability and control, with lots of structure and process. An "adhocracy" culture, in contrast, is more dynamic, entrepreneurial, and risk oriented. Again, there is no one right category of culture. Still, using these models to better understand your present culture, and how well it fits your mission, goals, and market situation, can be another important step in developing the culture that will serve you best at this point in time.

Just as for the earlier step of assessing culture, HR can play a strong role in pursuing efforts to identify the ideal cultural elements for your organization. Having managers commit to supporting the process and leading related decision-making is paramount. Even the process by which your organization decides on optimal cultural features provides insight into whether democratic processes (like voting) or more top-down decision-making are used.

Building the Right Culture

Todd Plymate, the family president of Plymate Inc., a commercial launderer, carries a few coins in his pocket at all times—not for vending machines or parking meters or anything that requires payment. In fact, the coins have no monetary value at all. Each has the company logo on one side and a list of the business's core values on the other:

- Do the right thing.
- Do it better.
- Image matters.
- There's more to life than work.
- Coworkers make the difference.

Whenever Todd observes an employee doing something that exemplifies one of the core values, he hands them a coin. Earning a coin is considered an honor within the company and a source of pride. It is a great example of how the business reinforces its values-based culture on a daily basis.

Once you have a clearer sense of the optimal culture for your firm, you can begin taking action to foster that culture throughout the organization. In building your desired culture, you are "operationalizing" your stated values. As illustrated above, culture has to be reinforced on a daily basis in everything the company and its employees do. This includes *don'ts*, or things the company should not do if it wants to align its culture with its values-based objectives. For example, if the business values long-term relationships with customers, then it cannot compensate its sales people with commission-only pay. Such incentives run counter to longer-term bonds between customers and employees. Offering a fixed salary component would reinforce a focus on relationships and longevity. Similarly, a business that wishes to express appreciation for the contribution of *all* of its people can reinforce this with a flat, less hierarchical organization chart and the absence of special top management perks such as executive dining rooms or special parking spots for family employees or senior managers.

The Canadian firm Kal Tire exemplifies operationalization of its values of respect, modesty, and long-term relationships. Founder Tom Foord is known for being humble to a fault, including bringing in experts to help with areas in which he has less knowledge, advocating highly decentralized decision-making (with autonomous, accountable retail store managers), and acknowledging that the company has been built on the abilities of everyone involved. The language used within the business also reflects its values and culture: employees are considered "team members," and meetings are "partner meetings"; headquarters is the "Vernon office," not the "head office"; the president (the founder's son) says, "I work at Kal Tire," not "I'm the president of Kal Tire." Every Monday, *everyone* at the business wears the blue-shirt uniforms worn by the store-based team members. Kal Tire also shares half its profits from the store division with team members. On an even more explicit level, at each Kal Tire store/plant, team members meet monthly to discuss how they have been carrying out the firm's seven Aims that define its culture. Teammates talk about what a given Aim means to them, and how they have used or will use their understanding to tackle challenges. These practices all help the firm convey, maintain, and benefit from its strong culture.

Here is a set of tips for building the right, values-based culture for your firm.

Do not start "right," just start: It is human nature to get overwhelmed by large-scale tasks such as overhauling a business culture. Too often, we let the "perfect" become the enemy of the "good enough." In short, it is better to start somewhere than never to start at all. So when it comes to consciously creating a desired culture, start small, maybe even with one symbolic item, such as sharing a values-driven story with the organization and building from there. Even the longest journey is made up of small steps, one after the other, and the first one is typically the hardest. This also fits with our theme of "constant evolution." Once you launch a culture-reinforcing element, it will likely lead naturally to the next element, and your actions will evolve as you incorporate new ideas and feedback.

Think day-to-day, not program-to-program: Culture-reinforcing programs or events such as new codes of conduct, town halls, or employee-recognition celebrations are important when used as part of a broader set of initiatives. But we think the most important factors related to culture are in your daily activities. How do people within the business relate to one another, customers, and suppliers? How likely are people to pitch in to help their colleagues, even if it is outside their formal responsibilities? The answers to these kinds of questions are found in the day-to-day of your business, and are more likely to reflect its true culture than any given program or event.

Get the leaders involved: Any kind of culture-building initiative will require the participation of the firm's top levels. If the leaders are uninvolved—or, worse, exhibit behavior counter to the desired values and culture—then it sends a strong signal that the effort is not to be taken seriously. In the best case, leaders embody the values and live the culture naturally, without conscious effort. However, when trying to shift a culture in a deliberate direction, some coaching and counseling of leaders is often necessary, to ensure that internal understanding guides external actions. Simple actions of top leaders, such as the language they use, their everyday behavior, and exemplary stories are very powerful. Here again, having leaders share stories that exemplify the kind of culture the organization wants, can go a long way. Leaders can send some of the initial messages about a cultural shift, and this can be reinforced and amplified by other people, communications, and processes.

Family participation is critical: Just as leaders in the business need to help set and cement the culture, so too do family members. Family employees are the best ambassadors of family values and should exemplify the culture on which these values are based. As owners and family representatives, they will be scrutinized more than other employees, providing both positive and negative examples. We have seen too many cases in which the family and business try to promote a culture based on respect and fairness, but family employees routinely park in "guest" spots or believe they are entitled to unrealistic compensation or special perks by virtue of their last name (for a more positive example, see the Box "When a Barbecue Is More Than a Barbecue"). Aim to have your family members serve as exemplars of the culture you wish to promote, rather than as poster children for "what not to do."

When a Barbecue Is More Than a Barbecue

The family owners of Vancouver-based Danica Imports have a longstanding tradition of hosting an annual barbecue with an important feature: the owners served the employees, as a way of saying "thank you." "Instead of them serving us, as they did with so much passion and skill during the year, on Company BBQ Day, the owners would turn the tables and serve the staff," said a first-generation owner. Rather than offering precooked food served on plastic plates, the owners grilled prime cuts of meat, serving these with fresh sides and gourmet desserts. When the upcoming generation suggested having Company BBQ Day *catered*, the owners balked, arguing that it was important for those in charge to serve the employees, as a symbol of their deep gratitude. They recognized, rightly, that changing this approach might subtly begin a trend away from their traditional strengths that included impeccable customer service and a policy of "always leaving something on the table" in supplier negotiations. The family owners of Danica understand that seemingly small actions can have big effects in ways we cannot always see. Employees who experience the care and service of their bosses at the BBQ pass that experience on to coworkers and customers, in many cases without conscious awareness.

Strive for "both-and," not "either-or": We have emphasized throughout the book that the most successful family businesses we have observed embrace paradoxes rather than avoiding them or ignoring them. That means they recognize the value of tradition *and* change, of family *and* nonfamily, of discipline *and* an opportunistic approach.

A culture of openness and flexibility will enable you to accept paradoxes and even harness their power more fully.

Do not forget the office and artifacts: Strong, conscious cultures are built on the visible and the invisible, whether observable features of the office or employee behaviors (such as cooperation), or that which cannot be seen, such as the dynamism and energy one feels in some firms. Kal Tire has laid out its corporate office in Vernon, British Columbia, to reflect its nonhierarchical culture: the executive team's offices are in the middle, with nonexecutive offices along the window walls. "There's glass everywhere for transparency," said the Retail Group's Senior VP Ken Chaun. "We don't have any secret *Mad Men*-type meetings here." See the "Culture Is within Your Walls" Box for an additional example. Similarly, carefully chosen artifacts can be effective reminders of the culture you want for your business. A great example is the giant Radio Flyer wagon outside the headquarters of the eponymous Chicago-based company—a 15,000-pound replica of the founder's original product, to exemplify the hard work that went into it and the next generation's respect for its past (the founder's son built the replica of the original, which graced the Radio Flyer booth at the Chicago's World Fair in 1893).[23]

Culture Is within Your Walls

When a US auto parts manufacturer's headquarters were flooded in the early 2000s, the family business took it as an opportunity to reinforce its culture of flexibility and open communications. The firm said goodbye to its mahogany-filled offices and created an open floor plan that made it much easier to work across groups and divisions. The family executives wanted to create a better way for the employees to collaborate, in line with its longstanding culture, and rebuilding the main office was the perfect opportunity. It is a good reminder that culture is literally within your walls (or in this company's case, the lack thereof!).

We asked family business expert John L. Ward, whom we mentioned previously in the chapter, what three tips he would give any family firm for building the right kind of culture. His suggestions are in the "John L. Ward's Three Tips for Building the Right Culture" Box.

> ## John L. Ward's Three Tips for Building the Right Culture
>
> 1. *Define the purpose of the firm, or its reason for being in business in the first place.* A surprising number of family firm owners, especially in later generations, have not thought through and articulated *why* their business exists—the purpose for which it was originally started, the purpose for seeking its continuity. Involving *all* owners in this process is powerful and essential to creating and developing conscious culture firm wide.
> 2. *Operationalize your values so that you can understand who will fit with your culture and who will not.* While many families have identified their family/business values, they may not have taken this next step to consider the beliefs and actions most consistent with their values (what specific behavior is most consistent with "respect," for example?). "Operationalizing" values with clear ideas/examples will help you hire the right people (both family and nonfamily!) to exemplify your values and culture, as we discuss in the "Recruiting" and "Selection" chapters.
> 3. *When selecting employees, conduct lots of interviews by lots of folks.* The idea here is that people carry culture, so the hiring process is essential in culture creation. A rich recruiting/selection process involving multiple people—ideally including family and nonfamily participants—increases the odds of bringing the most effective culture-bearers into your firm.

Ongoing Assessment

Culture is an ongoing process, a moving target, something that evolves constantly through the actions and choices of individuals in an organization. Once you have a culture that reflects your values and supports the achievement of your goals, you need to treat it with great care and appreciation. Take time to check in regularly on the state of your culture—both to ensure it is what you want it to be and to understand how it may need to evolve in response to changes in your business and family situation and needs.

The measures you can use to assess your culture are the same ones we discussed previously for understanding where you are, culturally, in the first place. They range from informal observation of activities and interactions in your firm to formal assessments conducted by external parties (firms like Human Synergistics, discussed above). For example, you can "audit" the fit between your actions and your stated values by using the Family Values Exercise described above. This exercise can gather feedback from employees and other stakeholders (board members, customers, suppliers, and others) to gauge what values the firm is "living" on a regular basis. Data-based feedback on your culture from this and other measures will be an important barometer for understanding where you are and whether you need to implement cultural shifts.

A commitment to the ongoing monitoring and evolution of your culture is more important than the exact method you use to assess culture.

The HR Function's Role in Culture

We believe that the HR function has a crucial, central role in making sure your culture reflects your values and goals. HR is ideally situated to help articulate elements of the desired culture, plan actions to perpetuate it, and help the organization live it in every way. HR's typical areas of responsibility—employee relations, compensation, performance management, and others—are prime contributors to a company's culture. When HR is aware of the direct connection between the policies and practices it fosters and the resulting culture, it can be an even more active player in shaping the culture most wanted and needed by all involved.

As such, HR can own elements of the culture of an organization, or at least serve as the firm's cultural steward—the previous sections reflect this idea. The challenge, as we have noted, comes when businesses do not value HR's potential for strategic contributions, and perceive the role as primarily administrative and/or "policing." HR, in such cases, is relegated to a "mall cop" role, versus the teacher, guide, and strategic partner it can be. While the family, the firm, and its leaders have some responsibility for seeing HR as a cultural steward, the group or department itself has to develop its own internal culture to serve in a more partner-like role. Ideally, all parties will recognize and reinforce HR's contributions to culture.

In fact, there may be an opportunity for HR to "fill the void" if family and other leaders have not or will not step up to the challenge of building an effective culture for the firm. That is, if HR recognizes a need for cultural change (or for preserving culture during a generational transition), it can promote this idea to leaders and others in the organization. However, if the business's leaders are attuned to the need for cultural shifts and monitoring, HR can help execute related initiatives in a strategic partner role. Either way, here are key culture-related activities HR can own:

- *Administer the surveys:* A natural role for HR is to run regular surveys that help the firm assess and understand its culture. HR people can work with other leaders and family members not only to administer the surveys but to help understand their results and culture-related implications.
- *Provide the coins:* HR can be in charge of creating or securing cultural artifacts and symbols, whether posters of core values, special coins for executives to give out (as in the laundry business example mentioned previously) or any other element. See the "How Vision and Values Travel within the Firm" Box for more ways in which the key cultural elements of vision and values may be conveyed.

How Vision and Values Travel within the Firm

- Posters or framed pictures
- Back of business card
- Brochures, booklets, handbooks
- Magnets
- Presentation footers, headers, etc.
- Oral and written communication
- Logos
- Mottos
- Program planning
- Systems and structures (e.g., recognition)

- *Keep an ear to the ground:* HR can informally track the firm's culture to assess how this lines up with where the business wants to be and its current situation, along with monitoring and trying to anticipate any potential crises that can damage the culture.
- *Challenge leaders and owners:* HR can be expected to challenge senior managers and owners if it finds evidence of programs or activities that run counter to the firm's core values and culture—such as a focus on short-term incentives in a business with a culture built on creating long-term value and relationships.
- *Ensure a match:* HR can be expected to ensure that HR practices throughout the organization are aligned with the business's stated values and desired culture. The function needs to have the courage to shift longstanding HR practices to be more aligned with the desired culture.
- *Keep it real:* HR can be the truth teller that listens to the words people speak, observes the actions people take, and draws a connection between these daily activities and the existing corporate culture. For operationally-minded leaders who see this as a side conversation, HR can make the case that culture is central to the customer experience and business operations, and thus a critical factor in company reputation and performance.

In this context, note that HR may or may not be a formal department in every firm; however, the idea of linking HR carefully to culture remains valid. At Canada's Kal Tire, for example, HR is seen as every leader's responsibility, especially at the store level. The store manager is responsible for creating what the company calls a "culture of accountability," which includes alignment with the seven Aims discussed earlier. The key idea is that everyone should be responsible for maintaining the firm's culture, which is supported and championed by the HR department if there is one, or the more general HR function, if not. In fact, culture is most powerfully experienced through direct, daily interactions among coworkers.

Beware These Pitfalls

Culture can be seen as an abstract or unimportant element in family business, resulting in a failure to take it seriously or address it strategically. Here are some of the most common pitfalls we have observed with regard to culture and HR in family business.

- *A negative mentality:* Some owners and managers believe they lack the means to develop a positive culture because they operate a low-margin business or are going through a period of lower profits. The reality is that culture is founded on values and principles, which require mostly nonmonetary resources and can be carried out largely through informal processes. A low-cost on-site happy hour that brings employees closer together can be as or even more effective than a black tie gala at a swanky hotel. Any firm in any situation can adopt many of the ideas we have discussed in this chapter to move toward a positive culture and all its benefits.

- *Failure to launch:* Starting is the hardest part, especially for something like culture, which does not have an immediate, observable effect on operations. So not surprisingly, many businesses do not get far with cultural initiatives, or do not start at all, focusing instead on more tangible issues. While this can result in longer-term negative consequences, the good news is that it is never too late to start. Just do it.

- *The middle management gap:* Your leaders may understand the need for a cultural shift and take real steps to make it happen. Your front line may already embody many of the elements of the kind of culture you want to have. But culture-focused initiatives often fall apart at the middle management level—or what could be considered your gatekeepers. Longstanding research shows a very real gap in the middle level of businesses, which can get in the way of real change.[24] Cultural initiatives and elements have to resonate with the middle, so think hard about ways to increase midlevel managers' engagement and sense of ownership. The best way we know of is pretty simple: ask them for their ideas on how to reinforce the culture. You will get better ideas than you would on your own, *and* you will get increased support from them when it comes to implementation—because they will feel a sense of ownership.

Things to Remember

- Culture in a family business is a dynamic, evolving business feature that can boost performance at all levels or become a barrier to achievement of strategic objectives. We define culture as resting on family values and comprising mutually reinforcing elements, including shared values and beliefs; behaviors, policies, and practices; and internal and external representations of the firm (such as artifacts and logos). Culture is a large part of family firms' success—including relative to nonfamily firms—and its role in HR issues is critical.

- We strongly advocate the development of a "conscious culture," including deep awareness of the firm's existing culture, an idea of what would constitute an ideal culture, ways to make the ideal culture a reality, and ongoing assessment of cultural features.
- *Awareness of your current culture* can be gained through surveys (general satisfaction questionnaires and those more specific to culture), group exercises, and third-party assessments.
- *Fostering awareness of the ideal culture* by relating stories that highlight the desired culture, by consciously deploying frameworks that promote your desired culture and by using an awareness of polarities to shape the culture in the desired direction.
- *Building the right culture* involves an emphasis on starting somewhere (rather than waiting for the "right" time), getting business leaders and family members involved, and not forgetting the visual/symbolic elements of culture, such as artifacts.
- *Ongoing assessment of your culture* can be carried out using the same tools you use to first gain awareness of cultural elements, including asking those outside the firm for their opinions/observations on your culture.
- The HR function has a critical role in building and maintaining firm culture, both through its typical areas of responsibility (such as employee relations and performance management) and its role as cultural steward. Key culture-related activities HR can own include administering cultural surveys, creating cultural artifacts and symbols, and ensuring leaders and owners exemplify the culture they wish their firm to have.
- Culture-related pitfalls include a failure to start the process of thinking about culture and challenges related to ensuring middle management understands key cultural elements and acts in accordance with these.

4

Recruiting

Midwest Metal and Manufacturing (MMM) was struggling. In the new millennium the company—which sold about $100 million worth of metal components to the automotive, agricultural, and other sectors annually and employed about 2,000 people—faced challenges related to its maturing industry and overseas competition. Demand for some of its previously best-selling products slowed, and rival firms, especially from China, made major inroads into its market share. Compounding the challenge were issues with talent: MMM was run by the third generation of the Meiner family, and while family members had led the firm successfully for many decades, based on strong values of quality, integrity, and people first, the current business situation's complexity was growing beyond their capability. Moreover, several cousins within the third and fourth generations had expressed interest in working in the business, and it was not clear how best to recruit such individuals, or even how to communicate potential job openings to them in the fairest way. In the past, the family had relied on word of mouth within and outside of the family to fill open positions, occasionally inviting college-age family members to be interns. They had also used a few informal guidelines for recruiting and cobbled together a page of qualifications when positions were open. These practices resulted in a strong bias toward bringing in the relatives of family members already associated with the business—and recently several, more distant family members complained about the bias. In short, MMM was being forced to explore better, more professional approaches to recruiting family and nonfamily employees, as part of its overall approach to successfully competing in increasingly challenging markets.

MMM, like many family firms, struggled with recruiting or identifying (and eventually hiring) the right people for the company. They needed employees who would create value by increasing financial performance and customer satisfaction, enhancing employee morale, and driving a cultural shift that would lay a foundation for future success.

* * *

Recruiting is the process of identifying the best pool of candidates and connecting with them in the most efficient and effective way. In that sense, the recruiting stage of the human resource life cycle happens even before an individual is officially part of the family firm. Getting recruiting right in any firm, family owned or not, is of great importance for multiple reasons.

First, getting recruiting wrong is costly. Hiring mistakes are expensive, especially given tight labor markets, leaner corporate structures, and, in North America, the slowly mounting retirement of large numbers of baby boomers.[1] The American Management Association has estimated that employee turnover can cost anywhere from 25 percent to 250 percent of the departing individual's salary, a figure that can add up quickly, especially for managers and executives.[2] Hiring mistakes do not occur only at the selection stage, when you actually extend offers to candidates. If you are not looking in the right places or attracting the right people to apply (or, conversely, attracting the *wrong* people), then you will fail to find the highest-value employees. Period.

Second, how a firm reaches out or makes itself known to potential candidates for employment will likely help candidates form their first impression of the company, influencing whether candidates choose to join the company and, if they do, how they feel about the firm's culture through their early (and even later) tenure. Recruiting practices also affect the general perception, positive or negative, of the company in the world, including as related to customers, suppliers, and the media.

We propose that the stakes of recruiting are even higher in family businesses for several reasons:

- *Most family businesses consider family members as potential employees.* This is especially the case for families who seek family leadership continuity—which is the vast majority of family businesses with which we have worked. A recent survey by the Family Owned Business Institute found that 80 percent of family firms intend to maintain family ownership into the next generation.[3] In many cases, family candidates have been exposed to the business in some form from birth, and may have been groomed for roles in the company for decades. Consider the famous Busch family behind Budweiser beer. They gave each firstborn son a few drops of the brew before he tasted anything else, including breast milk![4] In other cases, families have done their best to *dissuade* next-generation members from joining the firm, whether to protect the business from a noncontributing employee or to prevent a family member from entering a career for which they have no passion. Dealing with such issues sensitively, including as related to recruiting activities, is critical. Failing to develop good practices for family member recruiting can damage family relationships and trust.

- *Many family firms treat employees as family.* Because family firms tend to treat employees more like family members, it is important for all stakeholders that the right people are hired into the company. They will benefit from being treated like family, while contributing their performance and loyalty to the firm.
- *Family businesses are prominent in their communities.* Family firms have strong reputations locally and regionally. Their names are featured on products, foundations, and institutions such as museums and community centers. Many firms have employed multiple generations of workers from the same family. So recruiting new employees has the potential to affect their local and regional reputations positively or negatively.
- *Values and culture play large roles in employee fit.* In family businesses, culture is carried by deeply held and highly personal family values. As such, the alignment of values and culture among employees and the organization plays an outsized role in morale and performance at the individual and collective levels. That means recruiting has to be informed carefully by these factors, to ensure fit.
- *Many family firms take a reactive approach to recruiting.* "We wish we had put more thought into this earlier," so many family businesses have told us in regard to recruiting, and we have seen too many cases in which firms simply do not invest

sufficiently—money, time, energy, effort—in recruiting and suffer the consequences. Part of the reason is that many feel they can find employees easily among the extended family and its network. Consequently, they take a more reactive approach to recruiting, such as scrambling to fill positions that suddenly become vacant for any reason.

This chapter is a way of jump-starting your thinking about recruiting, by presenting in detail the issues you will face in recruiting for your firm, as well as strategies for getting recruiting right and pitfalls to avoid. In short, we want to provide you with thinking and tools to take a more strategic, *proactive* approach to recruiting.

A Reverse-Funnel Approach to Recruiting

Typical approaches to recruiting depict the process as funnel-like. There is a large universe of potential candidates out there—any adult in the world, in theory—and your job is to use a series of criteria to rule out the vast majority, eventually arriving at a small number to screen more carefully, interview (or put through a series of interviews and other assessment exercises), and hire. We think of recruiting a bit differently for family firms. In fact, we turn the funnel approach on its head.

Our "reverse-funnel" approach (see Figure 4.1) emphasizes the up-front thinking—discussed in more detail in the "Our Model" chapter—required to understand which types of candidates are the right ones to consider in the first place and then opening up the process to consider potential employees. That means asking important questions about what is best for the family and the business along several dimensions, and then using the answers to identify potential candidates and future employees from two pools:

- *Family candidates.* Approaching this pool involves not only attracting family members who may fit well as employees and providing them with the right roles and incentives but also potentially managing the expectations of family members who are interested in employment, but may not represent a good fit to join the firm in that capacity (though they may fit other roles well).

- *Nonfamily candidates.* Recruiting nonfamily candidates who may fit well involves understanding what makes a good potential employee, especially with regard to values and culture alignment, and strategizing about where to find such candidates.

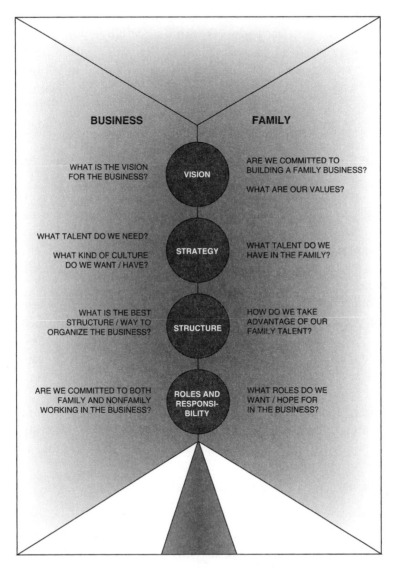

Figure 4.1 "Reverse-Funnel" approach to recruiting.

We believe that HR can and should play a strong role in recruiting—from helping the family understand how its values and culture should influence the process to managing the wide-ranging expectations of family members with regard to roles and responsibilities, well before any official "hiring" process begins. The foundation of our model of recruiting has actually been covered earlier in the book, when we discussed our overall model of human resources in family business and how each process within it should be informed by an understanding of key business and family issues, including vision, values, strategy, and structure. Simply put, you need to ask multiple key questions about your family and business before placing a single ad or reaching out to a single candidate. Please refer to the "Our Model" chapter for more detail, as it should form the foundation of your approach to recruiting and any other HR process.

On the one hand, recruiting may be viewed as a "numbers game," such that the wider you cast your net, the more candidates you will find, making it more likely you will identify at least one you would like to hire. On the other hand, it benefits no one to carry out a search that is much larger than it needs to be, burning through resources unnecessarily. So the goal is to engage in the most *effective and efficient* recruiting process, with focus on both family and nonfamily candidates.

Some family firms place great priority on recruiting and selecting family members. Others resist the idea of hiring *any* family members at any level. Each firm may have its reasons for a bias in one direction or the other, and while some of those reasons may be valid, we propose that relying excessively on family or nonfamily recruits is hazardous.

First, consider the example of an overfocus on hiring family. Research on family business shows that the majority of family successors are not adequately prepared for their roles, leading to lost value on multiple dimensions.[5]

What Do Family Firms and the Olympics Have in Common?

We, and others, have observed that family businesses are often biased toward hiring the next generation to manage their firms and assets.[6]

While that is understandable, it can be hazardous. In fact, Warren Buffett has said that relying on one's children as sole stewards of family assets is like choosing future Olympic athletes only from among the children of proven Olympians![7] The point is that such a focus would overlook many others who have strong capabilities, whether as Olympic athletes or family business managers.

Understandably, many families are passionate about having younger generations take over key roles, leading to questions like "Can we have *different* qualifications for family members?" This question is sometimes code for "Can we hire family members who aren't as qualified as nonfamily candidates?" The challenge is that even thinking about hiring clearly unqualified family candidates is not only harmful to the business but it also sends a dangerous message to other employees—that they are part of a system that is not merit based—and can reduce their motivation to perform, jeopardizing operations and survival long term. It also sends a negative message to family members and other stakeholders about what family business stands for. Such practices can ultimately erode the business on every level: culture, values, performance, and reputation. On a more practical note, sometimes there just are not enough family members to consider recruiting for key roles for the business, especially if it is growing fast.

However, the wholesale avoidance of recruiting family members is also potentially problematic. Especially in later-generation family businesses, there may be a group of members with strong competencies and qualifications aligned with the firm's needs. A no-family-hires policy can unfairly exclude such candidates. Second, and more importantly, failure to consider family talent means missing out on potential employees who may be deeply familiar with the family's values and culture, the people who can help carry these key features across the broader organization and into the next generation.

So we believe firmly that the best recruiting solution aims for a mix of family and nonfamily employees and executives, as long as candidates represent the right fit. As with many things in family business, it is not about seeing it as "either family or nonfamily" as much as it is about embracing the paradox of "qualified family *and* nonfamily." We also want to emphasize that even though the family and nonfamily candidate pools are separate by definition, the recruiting approaches to them are related, and each should inform the other. This is part of our general message that one important responsibility HR holds is to integrate family and outside talent in the most value-generating way for all parties.

With this in mind, let us explore each potential source of talent, recognizing that the best recruiting approach is *not* one that is rule- and policy bound, but one based in flexible practices that can evolve through experience. Think rubber, not porcelain.

Within the Family

Consider two examples of the recruitment of family members into the business. First, a California-based entrepreneur with holdings including car dealerships and insurance offices decided it was essential to have the next generation involved in the business, so he exerted great effort to make it happen. Part of his rationale was that he had worked so hard when his children were younger that he was anxious to develop stronger relationships with them as adults and colleagues as they worked together in the family business. He also recognized that involving the next generation in this way fit well with their interests and qualifications, so it was likely a mutually beneficial idea.

Second, the fourth-generation owner/operator of a midsized Midwest retailer recognized it did not make sense for any of his children to join the business. None of them had demonstrated the interest, through a number of experiences that included company internships supervised by nonfamily members. The owner/operator was very open with his children about the importance of doing work that matches with skills and interests, and over the years made sure they did not confuse a failure to recruit them to work in the business with a lack of respect or affection for them. His thoughtful approach helped ensure next-generation members found their right paths in life, without being limited by being required to work in the business.

These two simple examples illustrate the wide range of possibilities when it comes to recruiting family members, even just on the dimension of the senior generation's wishes and perceptions. In general, bringing family members into a business is simultaneously a highly rewarding and a tricky talent recruitment process. There may be nothing more satisfying than seeing next-generation members flourish in roles that add value to the family firm across dimensions. No matter what driver starts the process, getting family-focused recruiting right requires deep, mutual reckoning and understanding regarding several questions:

- What shared family values and objectives for the firm's culture will shape the recruitment of family members and nonfamily employees?
- What preferences does the family have for employing family members, nonfamily employees, or some combination?
- How will the family and the business promote fairness in the recruiting of family members, such as among siblings or cousins?
- What, if any, positions are family members excluded from holding?
- What roles do family members want or hope for in the enterprise?
- How will family members be evaluated to determine whether or not they are qualified?

The answers to these questions and similar ones will of course vary with each family's situation, preferences, and characteristics. To help guide your thinking about recruiting family members effectively, we offer several key success factors to consider.

Key Success Factors

Thinking carefully about each of the factors below (in no particular order) will help you take a more thoughtful approach to recruiting family members, increasing your chances of success. Note that we see these as dimensions rather than specific "targets" to hit or a rigid formula for successful recruiting. Use the factors below, along with the family business' history, goals, vision, and values, to guide recruiting-related decisions. HR can help guide thinking and decision-making related to the process, as well.

- *Clarity.* Creating clarity on what the family wants, partly through the development of guidelines for the hiring process, is essential to inform the way in which family members are recruited. For example, agreement on the desire for continued family ownership may drive an emphasis on early identification of potential next-generation family leaders. Clarity on the family's culture and values is essential for targeting ideal candidates, as well, to ensure alignment. There also needs to be clarity on the open positions within the company, such as information identifying the reporting structure and qualifications within a written job description. We discuss these in more depth in the "Selection" chapter.

- *Guidelines.* The presence of specific guidelines for family-related recruiting goes a long way to enhancing the recruiting process and its outcomes. This includes, but is not limited to, qualifications required or recommended to work in the business (such as an advanced degree and outside work experience), ways in which the extended family can learn about open positions, and how family members enter the business (such as interviews and application materials). For larger, more complex families, this will likely mean clearly written policies, while for smaller, less complex families, recruiting guidelines are usually present more as unspoken expectations of qualifications and/or behavior, but the core idea is to gain clarity on expectations through some means.

- *Boundaries.* Families that understand the need for good boundaries and maintain these can make recruiting-related decisions more easily. Boundaries are primarily about contact and interaction: who can and should say what to whom, including as related to decision-making. For example, how should interactions and communications around potential hiring of family members be limited and/or managed among the three types of family business constituents: family members, managers, owners? Clear boundaries, regulated by the different types of guidelines mentioned above, can help families navigate multiple recruiting challenges.

- *Access.* Unequal or unfair access to recruiting-related information and opportunity sets the stage for ineffective recruiting and broader erosion of morale and performance. This may take the form of enhanced access to opportunities for those whose parents work in the business or who live closer to headquarters. Some of this behavior is to be expected, but when access is extremely asymmetrical or characterized by "special favors" (such as an invitation for the CEO's son to open a plant in the south of France), negative outcomes are more likely. In contrast, families that promote equal access tend to enjoy better recruiting and performance outcomes. One family we know levels the playing field by having HR inform all family members of any open positions using a dedicated e-mail list. Others rely on mechanisms within the Family Council structure for such communication.

- *Transparency.* Transparency is related closely to several of the dimensions noted so far, including guidelines and access. Making information available on how recruiting takes place helps family members trust the process and feel more inclined to involve themselves in it—or to recognize that they may not be the best fit for a role in the business at a given time.

- *Formality-Informality Balance.* Family firms often take an approach that is too informal toward recruiting. That can be a mistake. At a manufacturing firm, the CEO tapped one of his three sons as his successor without involving the others in the decision. Fortunately, the would-be successor suggested a fairer process that gave each member of his generation a chance to be considered. Excessive informality can also lead to the family candidate being misled or taken for granted. It is not about adding layers of bureaucracy, but about implementing a sufficiently formal process that fosters transparency, trust, and fairness in recruiting.

Finding Family Recruits

Part of effective recruiting in family firms is creating a range of real opportunities to involve family members in the business. This allows for a deeper understanding of the business on the part of the family members and a mutual appraisal process. It is about determining the quality of fit in both directions. We have seen a wide range of formal and informal tactics toward engaging family members.

Internships can be very valuable to understanding fit before extending a formal employment offer. We have observed that more flexible, sometimes open-ended internship opportunities can provide great value to all parties. Developing a good internship takes a lot of work. Decisions must be made about

- the desired outcome of the internship experience;
- the possible roles and responsibilities for individuals at varying ages (middle school to college) so that the internship is substantive but not overwhelming for the intern;
- the level of compensation, if any;
- the specific learning goals involved; and
- who is responsible for managing the intern day-to-day, review criteria, and how frequently the person will check in with the intern

At a Midwest retailer, several family interns were recruited to work on multiple projects including business-related ones and development of a written family history. They met as a group weekly with a nonfamily point person who helped them learn as much as possible about the company and their position. At a Canadian manufacturing firm, a third-generation member with several years of outside engineering experience joined the business for a summer internship while earning his MBA. Such experiences help the family and individual members understand the viability and value of a more permanent role with the enterprise. Again, HR is an ideal resource for helping develop the right kind of experience for all stakeholders.

Rotational programs afford family members exposure to multiple parts of the business. These may be part of formal offerings such as internships, or may be provided on a more informal basis for multiple purposes. At agricultural company Ball Horticultural, the third-generation owner/operator's daughter rotated through the business on multiple projects, even though no formal decision was made regarding her future management role. The thought was that, whether she works in the business or not, she will be an owner, and the rotational program helps her be a better shareholder. So while rotational programs can be great for assessment of fit and potential succession—or typical recruiting objectives—they may also provide exposure for other important purposes as well, such as preparing next-generation owners.

Other tactics include *family meetings, facility tours, board meeting observation*, and *"family universities"* (where members learn about the family and business, their history, and business principles, in general). Each of these provides ample opportunity for the family and management to understand the interests and capabilities of next-generation members, and for rising members to assess their interest in the enterprise and potential roles within it.

Recruiting at the Dinner Table

Even simple dinner table conversations can be a means of understanding fit, culture, and values, helping to identify potential next-generation employees. The family of Holiday Inn founder Kemmons Wilson was known to enjoy "Sunday Night Suppers" together as a way to "keep the family connected."[8] Similarly, the family behind a Midwest clothing retailer shared a "Big Family Dinner" (they called it the "BFD") several times a year, presided over by early-generation members. At these dinners, every family member (even toddlers!) was asked to share their interests and ambitions, whether related to the family business or not. These dinners likely served as important *two-way* sources of information, helping the family understand which members made sense as potential recruits for business and/or governance roles, while also helping members identify their interests and aspirations.

Characteristics of an Ideal Family Candidate

The ideas above provide a framework for thinking about recruiting, including developing programs to help determine fit before formal employment. But the framework cannot tell you what makes an ideal family candidate. One challenge is that the senior generation (the parents) may have a biased view of their children, seeing them in an unrealistically positive or negative light. It is important for the family and HR to work together to develop a more objective view of family members' fit and potential value, as part of recruiting activities.

How do you determine what it means to be qualified? More and more research suggests that it is not so much specific experience and skills that matter when predicting performance, but character and potential. A recent *Harvard Business Review* article defines potential as the ability to adapt to changing business environments and grow into challenging roles, as suggested by candidates' motivation, curiosity, insight, engagement, and dedication.[9] The best family and nonfamily candidates should demonstrate those qualities in business and outside domains including sports, arts, military, and community service.

We have seen firsthand evidence of the value of potential, along with the predictive power of several other qualities for both family and nonfamily candidates:

- work ethic
- appreciation for family values, culture, history, and legacy
- long-term focus (at many family businesses, younger-generation members are encouraged to "think about their grandkids" when making career decisions)
- putting others first
- versatility, or the ability to work across multiple types of settings and challenges

Beyond Employment

We need to point out that the family is a potential source not only of employees and managers, but also of owners with other functions vital to the enterprise, such as leading the family council or charitable foundation—in other words, the "family" part of the family business. We know of many family business members, across generations, who lacked the interest or qualifications for roles within the business but have added tremendous value to their enterprises in governance-related or other roles. Here, too, HR can play a strategic role in helping leaders understand who is most qualified for specific roles that will contribute to the enterprise's performance, impact, and longevity.

Outside the Family

In our experience, early recognition of the need for outside talent and employment of a blend of qualified family and nonfamily employees predicts success, because a family has determined that they need a specific competency or experience set that is unavailable within their ranks. They know when their "baby" (the business) has outgrown the owner's capabilities in terms of scale or sophistication, or when their growth goals are too large for the family to handle on its own. Bringing in outside talent reflects openness to actively seeking new and potentially challenging strategies, mind-sets, and perspectives. And they recognize that having senior leadership comprised only of family members leads to limited diverse thinking, potentially promoting groupthink or the tendency of group members' opinions and ideas to converge. As is well known, some of the most successful family firms have nonfamily members in top management and board roles, with about 12 percent of family businesses having had nonfamily CEOs.[10] At the same time, some families have had negative experiences with nonfamily talent, so they tend to avoid recruiting outsiders into leadership roles. As discussed earlier, we suggest that erring on either extreme is a mistake. For example, trusting only family members to handle key issues—such as financial matters—is hazardous, but placing too much trust in experienced outsiders is equally risky.

The key success factors mentioned earlier for recruiting family members apply to targeting nonfamily candidates as well, with modifications as necessary. For example, guidelines and a balance of formality and informality are important in thinking about nonfamily recruits, but there may be less sensitivity required for determining who should have access to job openings than that required for family recruits.

Finding Nonfamily Talent

Some of our earlier advice for identifying family talent applies to nonfamily candidates, as well. At the lower levels of the organization, internships can provide great trial runs for potential employees from outside the family. At higher levels, we have seen strong recruiting results from approaching academic centers focused on family business (such as those at Northwestern University's Kellogg School and Loyola University). Graduates of these programs have been exposed to best practices and pitfalls in family business and are equipped with more realistic expectations about working in a family firm, helping to boost their contributions. Other potential sources of proven executive talent include structured forum groups (such as Vistage, MacKay CEO forums, and TEC), which gather senior leaders from across industries into small peer learning and mentoring groups, and organizations like the Young Presidents' Organization (YPO), which includes over 22,000 CEOs under age 45 across over 400 chapters worldwide.[11] While these groups may not be direct recruiting sources per se, affiliation with them can certainly help identify potential hires (within and outside the group), especially for higher-level positions. Potential board directors may be targeted through director-focused programs such as the United States' National Association of Corporate Directors (NACD) and Canada's Institute of Corporate Directors.[12]

The right recruiting approach typically includes a mix of formal and informal processes. Job listings may be placed on *employment-focused websites* such as Monster, CareerBuilder, Glass Door, and The Ladders. While these sites have a wide reach, they may also generate a flood of resumes, resulting in much more noise than signal. Some family businesses use contingent or executive *recruiters* who specialize in placing people into jobs within specific industries or business roles. The trick here is to find specialists who have access to relevant fields and candidates, along with an appreciation for what makes family businesses different. Some family firms have honed their recruiting skills by seeking high-potential candidates from *less traditional sources*. For example, the president of a Midwestern construction business travels to community colleges regularly to find strong recruits. He knows the traits that help entry-level employees grow into successful project managers, understands the high cost of training such individuals, and seeks out recruits who have those skills by getting to know them personally at college career fairs and other events. The firm also uses internships and summer jobs to further test potential fit.

Networking is one of the most successful routes to potential hires. According to the US Department of Labor, 48 percent of all job seekers, or a little less than half, secure a position through networking, or good old word of mouth: they cast a net using the people and groups they know.[13] Family firms can do the same thing. For family businesses, word of mouth can be ideal because it is likely to lead to candidates who fit with the business culture and values. Nevertheless, you must be very careful when recruiting candidates through this route, because the expectation on both sides will be higher, and there is greater potential for reputational and relationship damage, for both parties, than there would be with candidates who come from other sources.

Regardless of how you approach recruiting, it is important to emphasize the positive aspects of working for a family-owned business, not only to find people who relate to the benefits but also to counteract some of the negative stereotypes around family firms, such as their tendency to rely on nepotism for advancement. As discussed previously in this book, family firms have been shown as superior to their nonfamily peers on multiple dimensions, including business performance (revenues, profitability, share price), values, culture, and governance. Family businesses are often much more loyal to their employees, as well, with many known for avoiding layoffs even in the most challenging times. For example, a Family Owned Business Institute survey showed that many family firms will cut family members' salaries and dividends before laying off nonfamily employees.[14] Showcasing these positive elements to potential candidates, whether through formal (job listings) or informal (word-of-mouth) communications benefits all parties. For these and other reasons, many nonfamily executives are excited to work for family firms and will seek such roles, as emphasized by Craig E. Aronoff and John L. Ward in their book *More Than Family*.[15]

What Makes an Ideal Nonfamily Candidate

There has been a lot of discussion about what type of nonfamily leaders fit best in a family business. Our experience suggests that it is best to take what may be a counterintuitive approach to considering outside candidates. Specifically, while experience and competence are important, we find that *fit* based on alignment with the firm's values and culture is often the single most important predictor of success. In short, you should look for potential hires, especially leaders, who demonstrate credibility in both the business and the family during the recruiting process.[16] We suggest starting a recruitment process by identifying candidates who meet this criterion (as long as they have the minimum experience and capabilities required), and then assessing their competence more carefully. In short, confirm values and cultural fit first.

In general, the most effective nonfamily leaders share several key attributes, some of which overlap with the list we presented in the earlier section on recruiting family members:

- *Previous experience working in a family business and/or an appreciation for the importance of values and culture in a family-owned business.* This is a big one, and it includes several related dimensions: appreciation that business is more personal in a family firm, and that decisions can be much more wrenching, grounded in the family's legacy; a longer-term view, with emphasis on future generations; awareness that business issues may require family communication and possibly input, and that there can be many shareholders with divergent interests and opinions that need to be, at minimum, acknowledged, especially in multigenerational businesses.
- *A self-confident team player focused on development of others.* Leaders of this type show a refreshing sense of empathy and humility (low ego), and tend to be self-effacing, placing the organization's needs above their own, while at the same time demonstrating significant capability and professional will. They also display a level of self-confidence that helps them avoid competing with the owning family. Jim Collins refers to such individuals as "Level 5" leaders in his book *Good to Great.*[17]
- *Genuine caring for the family.* Such candidates show authentic regard for the family, resulting in heightened intimacy.
- *Superb communication skills* within and across boundaries— with family, owners, managers, employees, and the board.
- *An ability to visualize and share what they want as their own legacy,* even as a nonfamily leader.

While seeking out these traits in nonfamily candidates, you need to inform recruiting with a deep understanding of your firm's culture. For example, if your business's culture is characterized by strong curiosity and scientific inquiry, as is the case for many life sciences companies, then looking for candidates at a local university, lab, or research center would make sense. If altruism is one of your core values, consider seeking potential hires who have demonstrated their commitment to this value in organizations like the Peace Corps.

What MMM Did

Recall Midwest Metal and Manufacturing, the company profiled in our opening example. Let us take a look at how they approached their recruiting challenges, to illuminate the ideas discussed so far. Recognizing the importance of recruiting, MMM took a year to develop a much more strategic and comprehensive approach to the recruiting process, led by the HR department in conjunction with family members and outside consultants. Several important features emerged from the work:

- MMM established *guidelines* for hiring both family and non-family members, including the requirement of three years of relevant outside experience and a college degree for family members, and "proof" of fit (from interviews and other sources) with the firm's values and culture for nonfamily hires.
- The company *improved boundaries, access, and transparency,* as represented in part by entrusting recruiting to HR and the third-generation family members actively working in the business (rather than allowing fourth-generation owners to make informal hiring decisions). MMM established an internal family website and digital newsletter that included open positions and qualifications required. The materials went out to all family members, including those outside the business and those who lived far from headquarters. Hiring decisions were made by the hiring manager without influence by family members, and HR provided basic, impartial information about hires to the family, especially for higher-level positions. Recruiting practices for employees and governance roles were also discussed regularly at shareholder meetings and the family assembly (to which all family members were invited).
- A formal *internship* program was created for both family and nonfamily recruits. The internship program was publicized at regional universities and within the family, encouraging all college-age family members to participate in this program.

- MMM hired its first *nonfamily CEO*, recognizing that the business's market challenges had grown beyond the family's capabilities and experience. To find the new leader, the firm used a specialist recruiter familiar with both the industry and the specific characteristics/needs of family businesses. The new CEO came from a related manufacturing sector, and the family knew through industry associations and word of mouth that he had a reputation for being aligned with their values of quality, integrity, and people focus (he had forgone his salary during the recession that began in 2008). The CEO was attracted by the opportunity to perpetuate MMM's culture and legacy as well as by the firm's minimal bureaucracy and the ownership group's support of growth and innovation.
- The firm also engaged in an *ongoing discussion of what qualities to seek in candidates*, facilitated by HR and tested by assessing new recruits and existing employees on several competency dimensions, values fit, and performance.

This approach helped MMM address its increasingly complex business challenges with enhanced strategy and tactics and stronger hires at every level. Importantly, it also helped the extended family feel much more comfortable with recruiting practices, and attracted several third- and fourth-generation hires that old practices would not have yielded.

Watch Out for These Pitfalls

There are multiple pitfalls that need to be monitored to be sure that you are getting it right. These are some of the more common ones we have observed:

- *Jumping the gun.* It is tempting to dive into recruiting at any family-firm stage without having sufficient infrastructure in place. A basic organizational chart and clear reporting relationships are good minimum starting points!
- *Falling into the saying-doing gap.* Families that say they have a clear policy around recruiting but fail to enforce it will often find themselves in frustrating situations. In a family-owned

manufacturing business, a third-generation member asked the family CEO for a position within the firm, and the CEO agreed, even though the family had a policy of HR reviewing of all family employment applicants. Though the third-generation "recruit" eventually worked out well, the circumvention caused short-term upheaval between the CEO and his siblings that could have been avoided with better adherence to recruitment policies that involved HR as an impartial, professional third party.

- *All in the family—or not.* We suggested earlier that some families focus exclusively on recruiting family members, while others avoid employing family at all costs. It is worth repeating that both of these extremes are mistakes, because it is important to align individual interests, skills, and competencies with a given role, whether those individuals are within or outside the family. A comprehensive recruiting approach that involves family and nonfamily candidates typically yields the best results.

Things to Remember

- Getting recruiting right is of great importance to family firms because they often hire family members as employees, treat nonfamily employees like family, and have a strong focus on values and culture—among other reasons.
- We suggest a "reverse-funnel" approach to recruiting: do comprehensive upfront thinking about your family's and business's culture, values, vision, and goals, and then apply that thinking to identifying both family and nonfamily employment candidates. Avoid exclusive focus on family or nonfamily recruits.
- Several key success factors can optimize recruiting *within the family*: establishing guidelines and clarity about employee qualifications, creating boundaries between business and family decision-making processes, and maintaining a balance of formality and informality, among others, are important. Inform family member about the business through internships, rotational programs, dinner table conversations, and opportunities for mutual assessment of fit, with emphasis on character, interests, skills, and potential. Bear in mind that family members

may serve important nonemployee roles related to governance, family cohesion, and family philanthropy.

- It is important to recruit *outside the family.* Networking, employment-focused websites, family-business academic centers, and structured forum groups can be good sources of outside talent. Ideal nonfamily employees tend to have previous family business experience, appreciation for the roles of values and culture in family firms, and strong empathy/humility.
- Pitfalls related to recruiting include rushing into recruiting without basic infrastructure in place and saying one thing (such as having a strict recruiting policy) and doing another (skirting that policy), causing tension and confusion within the family and the business.

5

Selection

In 2004, family-owned Kwik Trip, operator of hundreds of convenience stores across Wisconsin, Minnesota, and Iowa, revamped its hiring process. Specifically, the company asked leaders of every division to describe the qualities their "A-players" (top performers) exemplified, and those responses were used to identify seven core competencies to seek in new hires. The first three questions of every Kwik Trip interview make clear the business's emphasis on hiring people who are long on character-based traits, rather than specific training or experience: "When is the last time you performed a random act of kindness?"; "Tell us about a time you treated others as you would like to be treated?"; "How have you made a difference in someone's life in the last three weeks?" Candidates who struggle with these initial questions are immediately out of the running. Kwik Trip's full selection process, which includes an extensive assessment—at minimum an online application, initial screening of candidates by phone, 1.5-hour interview, and reference checks—and careful communication of hiring decisions within the organization, is part of a culture that has helped lead to nearly 120,000 applications for about 4,000 open positions/year, with annual turnover of only 1 percent at the corporate level and a retention rate four times the industry average for frontline employees. Kwik Trip's hiring process has also supported and preserved the corporate culture that has yielded the firm top honors on multiple lists of Best Companies to Work For, at the state and national levels.

* * *

In the last chapter we discussed approaches to recruiting, or practices for identifying and attracting the right candidates to consider hiring for your business. Here we turn to the next phase of the human resource lifecycle: *selection*, or the process of choosing candidates to whom employment offers are extended, and the communication of the decision to the candidate, the broader organization, and other stakeholders including the owning family. The decision to hire a candidate represents both an explicit and implicit contract by which the candidate becomes a member of your organization, with each party maintaining specific obligations to the other. In return for specific compensation and benefits, the new employee will deliver performance that is anticipated to meet or exceed the business's expectations. Selecting the right employees to hire is one of the more important and powerful actions a company can make. Kwik Trip, discussed throughout this chapter, is a great example of a family business that has gotten selection right, yielding benefits for the business, its owners, employees, and customers.

Getting selection right is critical because the business's performance depends overwhelmingly on the performance of its employees. While recruiting helps identify the best pool of candidates to choose from, the qualifications, capabilities, and dedication of individuals within that pool will vary widely—as will their potential contributions to your firm—so selecting the right ones requires a thoughtful, strategic approach. What is more, once you make a decision to hire a given candidate, the stakes rise dramatically. Not only is there now a contract in place, whether literal or figurative, but "unhiring" (that is, firing) someone at any point in their tenure can be a very difficult process with large financial, legal, and emotional costs for multiple parties.

As discussed in the "Recruiting" chapter, employee turnover can cost up to 250 percent of the departing individual's salary.[1] The economic damage of bad hires can be staggering. Tony Hsieh, founder of Zappos, estimated that his bad hires (and their bad hires, in turn) could have cost the company over *$100 million* over 11 years![2] Granted, many of the people in question were top executives on Hsieh's team, with large responsibilities for strategic and financial decision-making, but the estimate underscores the importance of taking selection seriously. On the more positive side, selection of the right people as employees, especially at the executive level across departments or divisions, places significant power and influence in the hands of people who can create significant value for all stakeholders.

The "Recruiting" chapter noted that identifying the right employees is even more important for family firms than for other businesses because

- family firms often look at family members as potential hires;
- family firms tend to treat all employees as family; and
- alignment of employee and firm values is often a key goal for family businesses.

Moreover, we have observed that family firms, based on their longer-term view, people-focused values, and strong loyalty to employees, tend to be much less willing to let employees go, even when the benefits of doing so are obvious. They often wait much too long. Of course, this is partly because firing Aunt Mary is more challenging than terminating a nonfamily employee. But because they tend to treat all employees as family, many family firms drag their feet on firing or demoting *any* employee, whether family or not. They, likely more than nonfamily firms, sacrifice the longer-term benefits of doing that for the shorter-term avoidance of pain, thus keeping the peace temporarily.

Most everyone would agree that it is much easier not to select a potentially underperforming employee in the first place than to hire them and then have to deal with letting them go. The challenge is identifying a potential underperformer in the first place. This challenge is compounded by the tendency of too many family firms (especially in early stages) to take a more casual, ad hoc approach to selection, where hiring decisions are made with very little formal process. While it is understandable that family firms take such an approach early on, when the typical focus is survival, many retain such informality longer term, which is suboptimal on multiple dimensions. For this reason, we suggest a much more systematic approach to selection, with several mutually reinforcing elements.

A Systematic Approach to Selection

A midsized family-owned retail company we know quickly hired a nonfamily CEO based on a board member's recommendation, two brief interviews, and the candidate's seeming fit "on paper." Big mistake: it quickly became clear the executive's style was poorly aligned with the preference of the owning family and the broader management team. Largely because of this, the company struggled to develop a response to mounting competition, lost significant value within a year, and asked the executive to resign. "We waited too long to take action," a family executive with that firm admitted. The example highlights not only the large potential cost of a bad hire but also the culprit behind such hiring decisions in the first place: a hurried, unsystematic approach to selection.

We recommend developing a strategic selection system with multiple thoughtful components. This has multidimensional benefits for the business and family:

- *Better hiring decisions.* As computer programmers say, "Garbage in, garbage out." Poor or absent hiring systems yield suboptimal hires and performance. So first and foremost, a better selection system (or the presence of any selection system at all) should yield better hires, resulting in the creation of multiple types of value for the firm and the family: economic, social, intellectual, and others.
- *Fairness.* It is helpful to avoid perceptions of unfairness from both family members (within and outside the business) and nonfamily employees. A systematic, standardized selection approach clarifies the process behind hiring-related decisions and diminishes the likelihood of perceptions of nepotism and other unfair practices. Beyond perceptions, such a system should result in hiring that is unbiased and objective, generating better results.
- *Improved morale.* Hiring the right people for your business improves the morale of those already on board by boosting collective energy, commitment, productivity, and performance. Hiring the wrong people, especially in leadership roles, discourages people and drains the organization of energy and hope.
- *Return on investment.* A good selection system may seem like a large investment, and it is, especially at first. But such a system will pay for itself many times over. It will generate better performance and value through better hires, as mentioned earlier. It will also yield more effective and efficient use of resources,

by making clearer the people and processes involved in hiring, rather than relying on a fragmented process that pulls resources from across the organization, with high associated costs.

- *Enhanced culture.* Hiring the right people helps ensure that company maintains the culture desired by ownership, as based on the family's values. See the "Culture" chapter for more on this important topic.

"If you want A-players, you have to create a hiring system that leads to a culture of preferred employment," says John McHugh, Kwik Trip's Manager of Corporate Communication and Leadership Development. A-players, in turn, drive benefits for the business at every level.

Still, some families will resist our suggestion of a more systematic approach to selection. After all, many have gotten by with a more casual approach to hiring for decades—forgetting that the goal should be more than just getting by. They may also be reluctant to develop a selection system because they are afraid of getting it wrong, it seems too complicated, or they feel that going outside the network of those who know the firm well will be unduly burdensome. Risk aversion can also be associated with family firms, as they are naturally focused on continuity and longevity.[3] While we understand such hesitation, we encourage you to dive into assessing and reworking your selection approach because we believe that it is more risky *not* to have a systematic selection process in place. A systemic approach will generate the many benefits described earlier, and will provide an example and motivation for approaching other practices in a growing business systemically as well.

In such efforts it is important not to let perfection be the enemy of good. Assume your efforts to improve your selection practices will be continuous and ongoing. That is exactly as it should be. With that in mind, let us consider the components of an effective selection system.

The five components of a candidate-selection system described below and illustrated in Figure 5.1 are important elements of the overall human resource lifecycle for family businesses. Ideally, executives and others within and outside HR can collaborate to develop such a system. Where appropriate, we have also included a discussion of how to think about the selection process for family and non-family candidates.

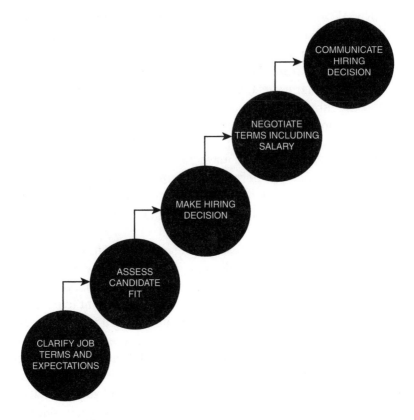

Figure 5.1 Components of a selection system.

Step 1: Clarify Job Terms and Expectations

Selection of candidates will be difficult without clarifying a position's roles and responsibilities and the prior experience and personal attributes required for a new employee to be successful. It seems like this should go without saying, but many firms get busy with recruiting and selection before clearly delineating the role and how that role will fit with others. Lack of role clarity is a common issue we observe in family businesses, and we suggest that the parameters to be considered should include the following:

- *Job description:* What is the expected role and related responsibilities? What kind of activities will the person be doing? What results are they expected to achieve? What are potential paths of advancement associated with the position?

- *Reporting:* Where does the job/role fit into the organizational chart? To whom will the new hire report? Who will report to the new hire? Here, it is also important to understand where family employees are situated with respect to the position in question. For example, when new hires report to family members, this may represent a potential "roadblock" to advancement. Or, the new hire might be expected to mentor a family member who is part of their team, who might also be interested in succeeding them in their role.
- *Compensation/benefits:* What salary range, bonus potential, and long-term incentive compensation (if any) are associated with the position? How do these compare with market rates? What benefits will be offered and how do these compare to the market?
- *Qualifications:* Given the terms above, what specific qualifications are expected of applicants? What minimal educational requirements does the position require and what would be ideal? What professional experience should the ideal candidate have and how long will the model candidate have worked? What proven skills and capabilities will the candidate need to demonstrate? What are the important values that you want to find in the candidate?
- *Assessment:* Though not a job "term" per se, it is important to understand how to assess candidates' skills to pick the best person for the position. What are the tools needed to adequately evaluate their strengths and weaknesses?

Thinking through these questions and any other relevant terms upfront, well before selection, saves a lot of trouble later—from identifying and hiring the right people for the position, to managing their expectations once they have been hired. Of course, there are no set-in-stone rules about exactly how specific you need to be regarding the terms. Like many of the concepts in this book, we see the definition of job parameters—and communicating them internally and externally—as existing on a continuum from highly formal to very informal. Where you should be on this continuum will vary considerably, based on the goals, geography, industry, stage, and culture of your business.

There are advantages and disadvantages to either end of the formality-informality spectrum. W.L. Gore and Associates, the makers of Gore-Tex (high-performance fabrics), for example, is well known for being very fluid in its approach to selection and other HR areas, based on the philosophy of its founder, Bill Gore. The company avoids job descriptions and titles, for example, and allows leadership (including the CEO position) to be decided mostly by peers, rather than management.[4] Thus a firm like W.L. Gore would likely do its best to find a place for strong candidates in the business, even if they do not fit an existing job description. While this approach may enable the firm to hire candidates they may have missed ("false negatives"; see the "Beware False Positives and False Negatives" Box for further discussion of this issue) because of overly specific job descriptions or qualification criteria, it may also result in hiring people who may ultimately fail to fit with the organization or the job in question ("false positives").

Beware False Positives and False Negatives

Families that have overly strict hiring policies—such as only hiring family members for top positions or never hiring spouses—may suffer from false negatives or false positives. One California family food business kept all family members out of key positions because past family employees had underperformed. That resulted in multiple false negatives, or the failure to hire several highly talented family members who could have boosted performance. Similarly, hiring family members for the wrong reasons (such as because they are related to the CEO) can result in false-positive hires who fail to have impact and may even detract from performance, culture, and morale.

Should the terms of a given position depend on whether it will be filled by a family or nonfamily member? Our philosophy is that families should strive to keep practices for selecting both types of candidates as similar as possible—in other words, to aim for a professional approach whether hiring family or nonfamily members. That said, we recognize that different considerations may apply to individuals from the family in some cases. For example, a family may choose to hire a family member with basic qualifications for a given position over a more qualified nonfamily candidate, especially if the family member in question has demonstrated potential and deep knowledge of the business's values and culture (as discussed in more detail below).

Step 2: Assess Candidate Fit

Assessment is about evaluating the candidate's fit with the specific position and the values and culture of the organization in general. We like to think of a candidate's potential, or fit, in terms of *competence* and *chemistry*. Competence concerns their ability to do the job they have been hired for—especially the "technical" aspects, such as crunching numbers for finance professionals or developing effective campaigns for marketing people. Chemistry is the "softer" stuff (which is often harder to see and quantify): can they get along with the full range of colleagues, customers, suppliers, and other stakeholders, and bring healthy levels of influence and enthusiasm to the work?

As discussed in detail in the "Recruiting" chapter, the current thinking on who makes the best hire has shifted much of the focus from specific competencies to more general characteristics and potential. In short, you are often better off going with the best "athlete" than with someone who may have extensive job-related experience or a specific job-related capability and less potential and uncertain character-based attributes. All of Kwik Trip's assessment processes, for example, gauge candidates on seven "core competencies," which despite their term for it reflect our *chemistry* component, with strong emphasis on character-based traits:

- work ethic
- passion
- high energy
- people person
- adaptable
- team player
- positive attitude.

"We believe you can teach specific skills, but your values are wired into you by the time you're 18," says Kwik Trip's communications head McHugh. "Those can't be taught, so that's what we look for."

We discuss Kwik Trip in more detail below, but also refer you to the "Recruiting" chapter for more about competence and chemistry, along with the specific attributes we recommend seeking among family and nonfamily candidates.

There are many specific practices and tools for the assessment of candidates, again ranging from formal to informal. Here are some of the more common approaches to assessment:

Personality and skills tests/inventories: There is a wide range of instruments that assess candidates' personality and skills. It is important that such tests be validated for a given use within the selection process, and that they are viewed as *supplemental* to the process, providing helpful data points rather than serving as sole determinants of a hiring decision. Multiple companies offer tests that assess candidates in multiple areas. For example, assessment firm Hogan offers a three-assessment suite including the Hogan Personality Inventory, which assesses people on seven scales: adjustment, ambition, sociability, interpersonal sensitivity, prudence, inquisitiveness, and learning approach. [5] A given profile may be more or less compatible with a given job or organization, when combined with the right specific competencies for the role. Similarly, the Myers-Briggs Type Indicator (MBTI) shows candidates' natural tendencies in four core areas: interpersonal focus (extraversion or introversion), approach to information (sensing or intuition), decision-making (thinking or feeling), and need for structure (judging or perceiving).[6] People's responses to the instrument place them into 1 of 16 possible personality types, such as introverted-intuitive-feeling-perceiving (INFP, for short). Specific MBTI types may be more compatible with certain kinds of jobs, cultures, or organizations. However, a note of caution: these assessment tools are not competency measures and therefore should not be used as the sole basis for hiring decisions.

Such inventories can be pulled "off the shelf" or customized to your organization with the help of testing-savvy consultants. Some businesses, especially in more technical fields such as software development, use skills tests to ensure candidates are competent in certain areas. As always, whether and how you use psychological or skills tests will depend on your specific needs, objectives, and philosophy. Note also that there are increasing legal constraints regarding the use of such inventories. For example, they need to be proven to reflect necessary skills or competencies for the position in question. So proceed carefully in this area, including consulting with your legal counsel as needed.

Interviews (or, "So why should we hire you?"): Interviews still represent the most common approach for assessing a candidate.[7] Interviews can range from an informal discussion over coffee to a grueling week of one-on-one and group conversations, from a phone screen to a formal presentation. Interviews are increasingly conducted remotely (especially in early hiring stages), using web-based technologies such as Skype, which allow for more affordable assessment of candidates at a distance. There is strong evidence that behavioral questions based on candidates' experience (such as "Tell me about a time when you successfully handled a past conflict between two or more coworkers") remain a good predictor of future behavior and performance.[8] Such questions may be supplemented by more hypothetical queries ("How would you handle a conflict between two coworkers?"), especially if a candidate does not have experience in a specific area. But these tend to be less effective than predicting success in a position than questions related to past experience. Firms such as DDI (Development Dimension International) provide businesses with tools and training to conduct interviews effectively so that interviewers can clearly understand the situation or task the individual faced, the actions they personally took, and the results of their actions.[9] Those details provide a solid behavioral example to predict future behavior.

Kwik Trip relies heavily on interviews, first using a structured 15-minute phone screen that assesses candidates' basic people skills. Candidates who pass through the phone screen are invited to a 1.5-hour interview. Even candidates for frontline positions such as store cashier are interviewed for this duration. "The length of our interview shows how serious we are about hiring the right people," says Kwik Trip's communication manager, John McHugh. The interviews include the three preliminary questions noted earlier—about random acts of kindness, treating others as one would like to be treated, and making a difference in someone's life—followed by three questions about *each* of Kwik Trip's seven core competencies noted above, for a total of 24 questions. For example, the questions related to the competency of "people person" are the following:

- Tell me about a time you showed empathy for someone else.

- Tell me about how you created an effective working relationship with your peers and/or supervisor.
- Tell me about a time you tried to understand other people's feelings.

Kwik Trip uses three questions for each competency to ensure that they have assessed the candidate's experience demonstrating the desired attributes, whether for a frontline or executive role. Candidates can draw from both professional and personal experiences in answering the questions, and the business likes to see evidence from both domains. McHugh notes that the "accuracy rate" for hiring—the likelihood of extending offers to the right people—has gone up significantly since Kwik Trip instituted its 24-question model.

As far as *who* should conduct interviews, it is usually a combination of HR staff, employees, and managers, depending on the business and the level of the position in question. Kwik Trip store or operations managers conduct interviews for frontline employees, and candidates for higher-level roles go through multiple interviews with several managers/executives. Here again the question of family involvement arises. We suggest having clear policies in place and keeping the process as professional as possible. For top-level positions, it is not uncommon and may be advisable to have candidates meet with family members outside the business, in addition to having interviews with the board and executives. After all, shareholders' economic status will be affected by the decisions of high-level executives, and finding a top executive with whom family owners are comfortable can be crucial. Providing training on how to conduct interviews effectively is an important part of preparing the interviewers to do their jobs effectively. Many organizations conduct interviewer training programs so that people can get comfortable asking behaviorally based questions and following up to obtain specific, useful data.

Internships and other experiential opportunities: As discussed in the "Recruiting" chapter, internships and other experience-focused opportunities can be a powerful assessment tool, giving all parties the means to assess fit. For example, MBA students typically complete summer internships with a variety of companies. In a family business context, interns can be family or nonfamily members, and they can be dedicated to a given project or function, or work across multiple areas during their tenure. Often, the intern's performance—as related to both competence and chemistry—provides a good basis for decisions about full-time employment offers, whether directly after the internship or at some future point (such as the completion of business school). (The "Recruiting" chapter provides more details on what makes an effective internship.) An important aspect of designing an internship program is to clarify up front the skills and competencies that you will be evaluating in participants and to ensure that you provide them with the opportunities to demonstrate their ability. It is also critical to make sure company employees are aware that they are charged with evaluating the interns' success.

Candidates at all levels may also be provided the opportunity to work on a special project for the business before being offered a job. Besides being helpful in assessing fit for possible future employment, short and focused projects or assignments can be ideal for the education of future owners. Such experience may take the form of supporting a communication initiative, conducting research on possible new product areas, assessing operational effectiveness in targeted areas, or many others, depending on the business's needs and the candidate's skills/interests. Candidates for higher-level jobs may be invited to participate with key employees in thinking through a tricky strategic or financial issue (that does not involve proprietary information), to get a sense for how they operate and collaborate. Again, these experiences provide highly useful material for hiring-related decisions.

Creative or customized assessments: Finally, the rise of new technology and the challenge of sifting through thousands of résumés have driven the development of more creative means of assessment. For example, some companies ask candidates to upload a brief video of themselves talking about their qualifications, interest in the company, or other topics, to gain a multidimensional view of them. Other firms may use a more traditional approach of having candidates write brief essays about themselves, their goals, and/or their interest in the company. An example from the academic domain is that Duke University's Fuqua School of Business asks applicants to submit "25 Random Things" about them in a list form, to help get to know candidates beyond their résumés and grades.[10] Finally, some companies (and candidates) may require a customized assessment beyond the personality or skills tests discussed earlier. Kwik Trip requires a drug test of all hired candidates, in keeping with the business's focus on strong values and performance.

To help compare candidates to one another, the results of the assessment process can be captured in a simple form like the one shown in Table 5.1, which is a modified version of an instrument used by a family business we know.

Table 5.1   Interview evaluation form

Candidate's Name: _____   Date: _____
Interviewer: _____   Position: _____
Experience Level: _____   Years of Experience: _____

Rating Scale: *(1 = insufficient skillset and experience for role to 5 = highly skilled and experience for role)*

Interpersonal/Leadership Skill Set					
1. _____	1	2	3	4	5
2. _____	1	2	3	4	5
3. _____	1	2	3	4	5
4. _____	1	2	3	4	5
5. _____	1	2	3	4	5
6. _____	1	2	3	4	5
7. _____	1	2	3	4	5
Technical/Professional Job Skills					
1. _____	1	2	3	4	5
2. _____	1	2	3	4	5
3. _____	1	2	3	4	5
4. _____	1	2	3	4	5
5. _____	1	2	3	4	5
6. _____	1	2	3	4	5
7. _____	1	2	3	4	5

Written comments and observations:

_____
_____
_____
_____

Recommended Course of Action:

___ Do not advance candidate   ___Advance candidate to next level
___ Hire candidate

Reference check: Reference checks are an often overlooked component of the hiring process. Some firms do not even ask for references anymore, given legal constraints on the referral source. Others ask for them, but do not check them before extending offers. Following up on references is an important way to confirm that the candidate's presentation in the interview and other assessments match their history of behavior and performance. For this reason, Kwik Trip has a policy of checking all three references carefully after the interview. "Verifying the references sends a strong message to our hires before they join the company," McHugh says. "If we didn't check, that would send an implicit message about our culture [that it's marked by low accountability]." While many family firms we have observed check references, not all do. Family firms also benefit from using their network to identify referral sources not provided by the candidate, especially for senior-level hires, to explore behavioral examples of a candidate's strengths and opportunities for growth. References are a great way to explore areas of concern that surface from interviews and assessment tools to determine the degree of validity.

Below we present a summary of the candidate-assessment tools we have presented:

- résumé
- background check
- personality inventories
- skills tests
- interviews
- internships or other experiential opportunities
- customized assessments
- drug screening
- reference check

Step 3: Make Hiring Decisions

To hire or not to hire?

That is the question you will face after defining job terms carefully and, hopefully, interviewing and assessing a number of potentially qualified candidates. Hiring decisions are especially important for family firms, for all of the reasons discussed earlier. While assessed competence and chemistry remain the most important components, it is important to note that family firms often take into account hiring-related factors that nonfamily firms do not, and that these can be important contributors to firm success. The hiring decision process is critical when related to family candidates. For example, sometimes the decision is forgone: the family wants to bring a talented family member into the business based almost purely on their observed potential and predicted impact. A Canadian retail firm created a position for the oldest second-generation daughter (after she had excelled in outside firms), assigning her to open a store in Boston as the first US operation. She not only launched a successful Boston store but quickly helped the business expand across much of the East Coast. Growing research, not surprisingly, supports the idea that the inclusion of family managers in the business helps the firm maintain its family identity and continuity.[11]

Similarly, families sometimes sacrifice a measure of competence for chemistry or look to employ family members who *collectively* represent needed experience or qualities. At a US West Coast financial services firm we know, the two sons of the founder are equal shareholders and deeply involved in the daily operations of the business. The older brother is the CEO, a very capable and talented professional, but one who is less skilled when it comes to interpersonal matters. He is all about competence, and could be thought of as the brains behind the business. His younger brother is in a lower-level position, and much less involved in strategic matters. But he is essential to the business because he is a very energizing presence in the company, one who talks to employees at every level and understands their needs and concerns. He helps his CEO (brother) take steps to improve morale and performance. As the embodiment of chemistry, he can be thought of as the heart of the business. Chemistry and the promotion of goodwill may also play a role in hiring less traditional candidates (such as those with special needs), whether from inside or outside the family.

Other factors play a role in family-firm hiring, as well. Sometimes the family takes seemingly illogical inputs into account, such as level of ownership (do those with greater shares get better shots at open positions?) and branch representation (do we need family employees from all branches?). The paradox here is that of inclusion and merit, and whether one should trump the other. As always, we respect the need for *both*, and understand that there are circumstances in which inclusion might supersede merit. But again we encourage you to move in the more professional direction over time, seeking to use both qualifications and inclusiveness to place people in roles that will help them make the greatest possible contributions while developing on dimensions that matter to them. There is growing evidence that positivity—or choosing to take an optimistic but well-informed view—in business plays a large role in success at every level.[12] In line with this, we encourage you to frame hiring decisions as positively as possible, focusing on what the candidate brings rather than what they lack. This approach helps breed success through the selection process. Stating the obvious, we would never advocate the hiring of an unqualified family member, but we would condone going beyond the competence focus to include chemistry dimensions where appropriate.

Hiring decisions can involve inputs from a combination of people within the company. Some families use a *family employment advisory committee* comprising members from HR, management, the board, family members, and consultants to oversee the selection and employment of family members. This special attention is most often warranted when there is a history of conflict or other difficulties with family employment. The diversity of skill and representation on this HR committee can help create a transparent, fair hiring process that fulfills all the terms of existing guidelines and policies, and minimizes the chances for family disapproval/complaints related to hiring decisions. Many times the family employment advisory committee is a function of the board's HR/compensation committee, which typically has responsibility for the hiring and compensation of top-level executives. In general, the family employment advisory committee can help "insulate" hiring decisions from the undue influence of family members. Such protection is even stronger if family members within and outside the committee recuse themselves from involvement in the final decision. This can include instances when the board is making a hiring decision about a family-member CEO candidate—it can do so using a committee of nonfamily members.

In general, hiring managers should be the ones with whom final hiring decisions rest. But decisions regarding key leadership posts may warrant more inputs, including from the family employment advisory committee. Also, if there are special developmental positions designed specifically for family members, the hiring manager may represent the final step in a process that has involved many others before him or her. In the vast majority of cases, final hiring decisions should be made by hiring managers, and it is ideal if they are free to select the person they most want in the job, rather than being pressured to select a family member or other favored candidate. In line with this, Kwik Trip endows hiring managers—at the store and division level—with 100 percent responsibility for hiring decisions, reasoning that the managers can identify the right people for their teams, and will be working directly with anyone hired. In general, the HR function can provide a more neutral perspective to help balance potential bias for or against family-member candidates, as well. Again the idea is to evolve toward as professional a selection system as possible, including who makes hiring decisions and how they make them.

Step 4: Negotiate Terms Including Salary

Hiring-related negotiation can be tricky terrain to navigate, especially when the candidate in question is a family member. Negotiation can take place around a large number of issues, including obvious ones like compensation and benefits, and less obvious areas such as professional development. Potential sources of tension include the younger generation's feeling that they are entitled to special compensation and other terms by virtue of their family membership, versus the senior generation's sense that new family hires should be grateful and accept whatever is offered. At a family-owned East Coast apparel company, the second-generation CEO felt that negotiating with a third-generation hire was unnecessary. The candidate disagreed, and insisted on requesting changes in the job terms. The issue caused months of upheaval among the family, as members took sides. Similarly, younger-generation members may feel they are being underutilized (such as being offered a job with little effect on operations or the bottom line) or marginalized, and it is important that the upfront negotiation include a discussion of expectations.

As a general rule, it is important to have some guidelines in place—whether formal or informal—for hiring-related negotiation. We believe it is important to implement company-wide policies that apply to all hires, whether family members or not. Any family policies can also refer to these, to minimize ambiguity. For example, every position, whether filled by a family or nonfamily hire, will have an associated salary range that is nonnegotiable. The table below contains examples of formal approaches to compensation policies for family members.

In general, "What would you do if this *weren't* your family?" is a good question to ask yourself as you develop your approach to negotiation. That can help you handle tricky negotiation issues related not only to compensation but also to vacation (will family employees be required to use their vacation to attend family business meetings and family trips, for example?), life insurance (will family members be offered more coverage than nonfamily hires?), and education (will family members receive higher education benefits, such as tuition reimbursement?). While there are no hard and fast rules related to policies on these matters, we encourage you to consider the collective good—including perceptions of fairness—carefully when making decisions on these issues. We encourage family firms to build policies on these matters in advance of when they need them. A sample compensation policy is included in the "Sample Family Enterprise Compensation Philosophy for Family Members" Box (Table 5.2).

Table 5.2   Sample family enterprise

Compensation Philosophy for Family Members

Our objective is to provide fair and equitable rewards to family members active in the business who execute their responsibilities and take a stewardship role in our family enterprise.
We will

- structure compensation with the ability to adapt to changing market conditions; specifically, keeping the fixed portion of compensation near industry averages and the variable or performance portion equal to or above industry averages;
- include a bonus and deferred profit sharing pool in which up to 25% of operating earnings, depending on financial performance, may be made available for distribution to eligible family employees; and
- provide other benefits in the form of vacation time, retirement contributions, and medical, dental, disability and life insurance programs that would be considered at a minimum "competitive" with similar companies in the area.

Step 5: Communicate Hiring Decisions

When two third-generation cousins of a Midwest automotive supply firm heard the firm's president announce at a shareholders' meeting that a third cousin had been promoted to an important VP role, they were understandably frustrated. All three had interviewed for the position, and the announcement was the first time any of them had heard the outcome. Communicating about hiring decisions is a critical but often overlooked process, one that can cause significant tension and resentment or set the stage for healthy acceptance and stronger performance.

As the example above suggests, the first line of communication should be with all the applicants. There are few application-related phenomena more frustrating than hearing a personal outcome second- or thirdhand, whether the news is positive or negative. No one beyond the hiring committee/group should hear the decision before the candidate does. Communication with the candidate can take the form of verbal offers (or explanation of reasons for a "no"), e-mails, or formal letters including terms. In-person communication is often best, though it can be difficult due to geography or timing. Subsequently, once the candidate accepts the terms, the board can be informed (especially for executive positions and family hires), followed by candidates who were not accepted, the broader organization, and the larger family. Ultimately, major hiring decisions can be shared in the family newsletter, in a special e-mail, or as an announcement at a shareholders' or other meeting, depending on the level of the hire. Kwik Trip, for example, communicates management-level hiring decisions—for family and nonfamily hires—through a daily e-mail and company newsletter.

When communicating with the broader family, especially about the outcomes of family candidates, transparency is crucial. Family members want to know who has been selected and why, and, especially when multiple members are involved, may want to know as much as possible about the process of selection. Careful communication is especially important in families that have a history of tension, rifts, and/or negative nepotism. The absence of information in that context is even more likely to lead to suspicion-fueled attributions, such as "If you're not telling me something, it must be because you have ulterior motives." When in doubt, *overcommunicate*. One caveat: details of employee remuneration are private to the individual being hired.

Constant Evolution of Selection Processes

Last but certainly not least, there needs to be an emphasis on constant evolution, not only for selection but for all elements in this book. Similar to terms like "continuous improvement" or "continuous learning," "continuous evolution" represents an ongoing process of applying new thinking and experience-based insights to existing systems in ways that bring both small and large changes. What works well? What does not work so well? What needs improvement? Whose input can you use to help get the system to the next level? Some families we know ask all applicants—including those who do not get the job—what they might do to improve their hiring processes. These and other inputs can help ensure that the way you select candidates evolves to address changing times, business situations, and candidate expectations. Evolve as if your business's survival depends on it. Because it does.

Pitfalls

Remember: making poor selection choices can have multiple negative consequences for the family and the firm. Here are common pitfalls related to selection.

- *Letting fear drive selection:* Families that have been burned by selecting the wrong candidates in the past may find it especially difficult to pull the trigger on hiring decisions. For example, hiring a nonfamily CEO who turned out to be a poor fit may make it difficult to hire another nonfamily top leader in the future. This can potentially lead a firm to overlook strong candidates. Similarly, fear of family disapproval can result in suboptimal selection, such as when a given family branch is especially vocal about their preferences. In all of these cases, the better route is to rely on as professional and objective a process as possible, using your stated values and applying more positive thinking, as suggested earlier in the chapter.

- *Overrelying on your gut:* Gut-based decision-making is especially a problem in the founding generation, as founders are used to doing everything on their own, including hiring. They may make key hiring decisions on a whim ("I just liked him") or for expedience ("We needed to fill the position fast"), and then quickly come to regret them. Of course, subsequent generations may also make this mistake. Intuition is fine to use, but should be supplemented by facts. Your gut can be fooled, especially by candidates long on chemistry but potentially lacking in competence. We make the case for using multiple inputs in selection, including the assessment tools we have covered, or similar tools, and the feedback of multiple parties, especially those with a strong hiring track record. These should yield convergent evidence to facilitate hiring decisions.

- *Putting candidates on a pedestal:* Families, especially those that have been through challenging business situations, sometimes place outside executive candidates on a pedestal, endowing them with virtually magical qualities while devaluing the family's or past/current executives' capabilities. "Once we hire Lucy, all our problems will be solved." The danger of such thinking is that it creates unrealistic expectations and can result in failure of the board or management to properly oversee the new executive, often resulting in poor performance at multiple levels. Managing expectations and working collaboratively with new hires at any level, regardless of their ostensible capabilities, is always the better route.

- *Blurring the boundaries.* It is easy to blur boundaries around hiring, especially those at the intersection of family decisions and management decisions. Endowing family members with excessive influence over who gets hired can wreak havoc in the business and the family. As we have emphasized, hiring decisions (of family and nonfamily employees) are a management and board decision supported by HR. These are the people who work in the business day to day and best understand its needs.

Things to Remember

- *Selection* is about choosing the best hires for your business, along with negotiating the terms of their employment and communicating the hiring decision to them and others within and outside the organization. Getting selection right is critical because employees drive performance and culture, and "unhiring" people is costly on multiple levels. This is especially true for family firms.

- We advocate a *systematic approach* to selection to promote improved hiring decisions, fairness, and morale. Effective selection systems include the components noted below.
- *Clarity on job terms* covers the job description and required qualifications, reporting, compensation, and means of assessing candidates' skills. The formality or informality of your approach to job terms should vary based on your particular situation.
- *Assessment* is about evaluating candidates' fit with a given position and the organization's values and culture. The two key dimensions of fit are competence and chemistry, with growing emphasis on the chemistry—or character-related—component. Assessment tools include personality inventories (validated and used carefully), interviews, internships, and customized assessments.
- *Hiring decisions* for family firms often take into account factors that nonfamily firms might not, such as placing a qualified but less experienced family member in a key role. We suggest considering both inclusion and merit for family member hiring decisions, with as professional an approach as possible. Hiring managers usually have final say in hiring, with input from HR and a family employment advisory committee as needed.
- *Negotiation* can be tricky with family members, so it is important to have company-wide policies in place and specific guidelines or limits in place with regard to family members, especially as related to maximum compensation. Again, aiming for a professional approach is best.
- *Communication of hiring decisions* should begin with the candidate selected, the board (for higher-level hires), other candidates, the broader organization, and the family, usually in that order. Transparency about the selection process is critical, especially when family members are involved.
- Selection systems and processes work best when they *constantly evolve*, with the application of new learning and insights from current systems.

- Selection-related pitfalls include letting fear (such as that based on past hiring experiences) drive the process, overrelying on gut instincts, and placing potential new executive hires on a pedestal, with the assumption that they will solve all issues.
- Here is a quick checklist (Table 5.3) for the components of selection identified in this chapter.

Table 5.3 Checklist for selection process

___Identify and prioritize key requirements of the job
___Develop job description
___Define salary range/compensation
___Determine reporting relationship
___Create job application (if applicable) & design interview questions
___Notify family and post job
___Review resumes and applications
___Design and complete screening/selection process based on job level (assessments, background check, drug screening, interview, reference checks)
___Evaluate candidates
___Draft offer letter and call candidate to make verbal offer
___Draft and send decline letters (if relevant)
___Communicate hiring decision and rationale to family, board and business

6

Onboarding

First impressions matter, and the onboarding experience is the most substantial first impression your company will deliver to new employees. In the "Recruiting" and "Selection" chapters we noted that how you treat people from the earliest stages (even before they are hired) will influence their experience and connection to the company and, in turn, their motivation to perform their best. It will also affect the perception of the company by other stakeholders, including customers, suppliers, and the broader community in which the company operates. In this context, onboarding, the next phase in our HR lifecycle and the most in-depth early interaction between company and employee, is where the "rubber meets the road." For example, a poor recruiting or selection experience for new hires may be offset by a thoughtful onboarding experience. However, a miserable onboarding experience will not only diminish employees' morale and performance but likely motivate them to head for the exit sign, permanently. And the cost of replacing valued employees is extremely high, especially for family businesses.

The scenarios below take you through hypothetical onboarding experiences at two very different family businesses:

Company 1: Nothing Right, Inc.

Before your first day, you receive nothing from the company, other than some standard paperwork to fill out for your background check. To confirm your starting date (which is fast approaching), you call

HR and are placed on hold for several minutes by an assistant who sounds bored. You are almost ready to hang up by the time he returns to the line. When you ask about your starting date, he says he has no record of you, and then places you on hold for an even longer period. Finally, he returns to the line and says, "Yes, you can come in on that day." Then he hangs up.

When you arrive for your first day, you recall several aspects of the business from the interview phase that you now see in a new light. For example, you find that the choice spots in the parking lot are reserved for business family members, as made clear by large placards bearing their names. A late-model luxury car occupies each of the reserved spaces, and the Visitor spots are also all taken by luxury autos. Yet when you enter the building, you are again surprised by the poor condition of the reception area: decades-old chairs and tables in disrepair, outdated magazines, and dusty plaques for awards won many years earlier. There is no receptionist, only an old office phone with a handwritten note: "Press 0 for service."

Eventually you are shown to your cubicle by a different bored assistant—and left there without further instruction, just a copy of the employee handbook and vague mention that your supervisor will come to see you "before too long." When it is time for lunch, your supervisor still has not arrived, so you enter the company cafeteria alone and sit by yourself. Several other employees join your table, but after briefly introducing themselves they begin a work-related discussion to which you cannot really contribute. You are hopeful that the next day will be better, partly because an "orientation" event has been promised.

Unfortunately, the orientation is not what you had hoped. You and three fellow new hires are shown to a cramped meeting room, where you hear a few perfunctory welcoming remarks by an HR person, followed by a poorly produced video about the company's history. After the video, the HR person asks you to fill out paperwork related to your pay and benefits, and then asks if anyone has any questions. "Why did I accept this job?" you think to ask. However, you do not.

Things do not improve over the first weeks and months. Your supervisor has assigned you a few tasks that you are clearly expected to complete on your own. While you are okay with autonomy, you would have liked more support for your transition, and the opportunity to ask a few questions. Moreover, it is clear that family members working in the business receive preferential treatment, from choice parking spots and project assignments to faster promotions (from what you hear from other nonfamily employees). Not surprisingly, this contributes to a sense of entitlement among family employees and clear, sometimes vocal, discontent among nonfamily employees. By the end of your third month there, you are not surprised that your supervisor has not checked in with you in any depth regarding your experience during the transition. Had someone asked, your honest answer would have been that you have not been performing your best, largely due to the lack of support, and that you are seriously considering leaving the company.

Company 2: All Right Co.

A week before your official start date, you receive a smart-looking "welcome package" that includes a guide to your first week at the company, along with several attractive samples of the consumer goods the company makes and several electronic links to information about the company, its values, and its accomplishments. As your first day approaches, you receive multiple calls from the company—HR, the hiring manager (your supervisor to-be), and the family-member VP of your division—to confirm your start date and ask if you have any questions or special needs to be addressed before you start. You are pleased to find they also ask about your interests outside work and even your favorite foods. "We're really excited to have you join us," each person says at the conversation's end.

On your first day, you arrive to find a parking lot with many open spaces, including the Visitor area where you have been instructed to park (for the first week). The lobby is a bright and airy room with the company's name and logo etched in glass, above an appealing, colorful display of company-related pictures and products. You are greeted by a smiling receptionist, and the sign on her desk says "Director of First Impressions." "We're so glad you're here," she says genuinely, and hands you a "First Day" packet including a map of the office (with your division and work-space marked clearly) and a brightly wrapped candy box with the company's logo. When you start to head to your office, she asks you to wait. "Your buddy is on his way," she says. Within minutes your "buddy" arrives: a peer from your division who has been assigned to help you find your way around for the first week. He, too, is clearly happy to help you, and he takes you to get your ID and badge, followed by a group breakfast within your department, an event arranged especially for you to meet your new colleagues.

Later, at lunch, you and your buddy sit at a dedicated table with several fellow new hires, their buddies, and other colleagues, including family employees, representing several levels within the organization. "We like to make sure you don't eat alone on your first day," the family-member VP of your division says. You and the other new hires are asked to say a little bit about yourselves, and you find that you have several things in common with some of your lunchmates, including where you went to business school and your favorite type of music.

After lunch, you and the other new hires are taken on a tour of the company by a family employee who makes sure to introduce you to as many people as possible. The group chuckles when she points out the deliberate misspelling on a plaque outside an executive conference room: "The Bored Room." Later, you attend an orientation event at which several helpful HR staff guide you through your paperwork and answer your questions thoughtfully. Two family employees arrive to speak about the company's history, values, and culture, and to ensure you have what you need to get started.

Once the work begins, you feel well supported by the company—from your buddy's helpful inputs during the first week to regular check-ins regarding your transition by HR and colleagues in your division. You are also pleased to see that, while everyone knows who the family employees are, there is never a sense that they are more important than nonfamily employees, with regard to assignments, promotions, or any other dimension. The company clearly has a merit-based compensation system. In fact, several family employees point out that they hold themselves to high standards for embodying the family's and business's values, and that all employees should speak up if they feel they are falling short in any way. At your third monthly check-in, you tell your manager that you hoped you would have a good experience with the company, and that your onboarding experience there has exceeded your highest expectations, motivating you to deliver your best performance.

* * *

It should be clear that the first example illustrates a suboptimal (to say the least) onboarding experience at a family business, while the latter depicts an exemplary one. Admittedly, we have written the scenarios as extreme contrasts to illustrate our point. But each element in both has been taken from our firsthand experience with family businesses—even the old reception room phone with the "Press 0 for service"!

The simplest way to highlight the importance of onboarding is to say, "The start counts."[1]

Multiple sources confirm the importance of onboarding.[2] For example, 40 percent of new executives fail within their first 18 months, a statistic that could likely be improved by a better early experience.[3] But onboarding is, of course, important at *every* level of your organization. As we have suggested throughout the book, the process is likely even more important for family firms than others, for several reasons:

- their focus on *continuity*, which requires high performance, strong morale, and low turnover
- their tendency to *treat all employees as family members*, which means they want to offer their people the best experience possible, from start to finish
- their *loyalty* to employees, which makes them reluctant to let go of their people, even those performing poorly
- their *prominence and standing in the community*, which makes maintaining their reputations and fostering positive employee responses paramount

For these reasons, we urge family businesses and those responsible for their HR processes to take onboarding very seriously. The first step to doing that is to cast off the old notion of onboarding as a transaction-focused orientation, and to see it for what it should be: the *integration* of new hires into your business on multiple dimensions.

Onboarding as Integration

"Orientation" is a more familiar term for what HR now more typi-cally calls "onboarding." Whether for new employees (including leaders and others), students, or volunteers, the orientations of the past involved early events that helped people get acquainted with their new organization—typically some form of "meet and greet," along with attention to administrative details such as HR paperwork, assignment of office space, and others. While those activities remain important for new employees of family busi-nesses, thoughtful firms have come to recognize that entering a company should be considered more of a *transition* than a series of transactions. Thus onboarding has become a longer term process that integrates employees more seamlessly into the organization through enhanced understanding of their roles/responsibilities (and how these add value to the firm) and the development of key relationships within the business through "strategic socializa-tion," or meeting the right people at the right time within their development.[4]

It is important to recognize that recently hired employees are becoming part of a system that is new to them, and this requires "two-way" adjustment: adjustment of the individual to the organiza-tion, and vice versa, as suggested by Figure 6.1.

Based on this perspective, we see onboarding as an *integrative* process, one that not only covers administrative issues but also ori-ents new people thoroughly to the firm's values and culture. Thus

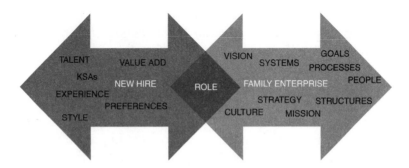

Figure 6.1 Onboarding as a two-way, integrative process.

Note: KSAs are Knowledge, Skills, and Abilities.

onboarding reflects a "conscious" firm's commitment to having each new employee start off on the right foot in the following ways:

- *familiarity* with and appreciation for the organization, its people, and its context (such as history and industry)
- *knowledge* of the business's offerings, structure, systems, and processes
- *positive morale*, in terms of feeling good about the firm, its mission, its people, its values, and its culture
- *motivation* to deliver high performance
- *better fit* into the business's norms and customs
- *an internal network* that helps boost productivity and morale
- *understanding performance expectations* on every level: responsibilities and tasks (assigned and others), leadership, interpersonal impact

Seeing onboarding as integration also means taking a longer term view. It is not just about the first day, first week, or even the first month on the job. It is about ensuring that your people are anchored firmly (and positively) by their early experience with your firm, convinced that the organization has their best interests in mind, and have an understanding of how they can add value. In the next sections we discuss best practices with regard to specific phases of the onboarding process (see Figure 6.2),

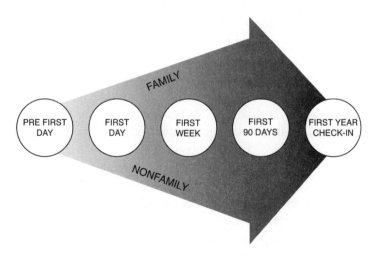

Figure 6.2   Onboarding timeline.

with practical tips related to new family and nonfamily employees, along with tips for onboarding leaders and other employees.

Before the First Day

When it comes to professional life, most people do not like surprises, especially unpleasant ones (like those in the opening "Nothing Right, Inc." onboarding scenario). So it is crucial to prepare your new employees for what to expect when they arrive at the firm, from the first day forward. That also means preparing the firm for their arrival, as part of the two-way-adjustment idea. The following questions are important to answer affirmatively and thoughtfully for *all* entering employees.

- *Do new employees receive anything before arriving?* As suggested by our positive opening example, there is a wide range of possibility here, ranging from check-in phone calls to welcome packets with information on culture, along with small product samples if appropriate. Because the owning family's values are so central to the business, anything that conveys these foundational beliefs will be valuable for the new hire. Many families do this in a powerful way, for example, by sharing a detailed history of the family's involvement in the company. While there is no set formula for prearrival materials, the bottom line is to offer something thoughtful that will help new hires better understand the unique values and culture of the family business, feel good about their decision to join the firm, and be energized to deliver high performance from the start. Personal contact, especially with family employees as well as their future managers and colleagues (including people who interviewed them), is particularly encouraging. Employee handbooks can be helpful; US convenience store operator Kwik Trip, for example, sends new hires information on expectations regarding the dress code and behavior before they start work. Developing a fun, accessible handbook is a good goal. For example, multimedia financial services firm The Motley Fool, though not a family business, is well known for its whimsical, irreverent culture, and has a fun set of employee guidelines available online.[5]

- *Is the reception area ready for new employees?* This may seem like a simple issue, but it is often overlooked. We have seen too many lobbies like the one in our opening scenario: old furniture, absent (or, worse, rude) receptionists, no company logo or other company paraphernalia. A clean, attractive reception area with meaningful company signs, symbols, and artifacts helps create the best first impression for anyone entering it, especially new employees. The front entrance to the corporate headquarters for Radio Flyer, for example, features the huge wagon that had been in the Chicago World Fair, symbolizing the firm's longevity and ability to "think big." The company's offices remain in its original building, but have been completely remodeled (with award-winning results) to reflect the business's design sensibility and commitment to sustainability. Similarly, the reception area of one of our manufacturing clients displays the founder's original toolbox from many decades ago, and its dents and scratches make clear the hard work that has gone into building and sustaining the company over the years. These and other reception area features help make new employees feel motivated to contribute from the moment they enter the premises.

- *Does the organization know they are coming?* As suggested by our "do not" opening scenario, it can be very frustrating for new people to feel their arrival was not expected. A lack of preparation in this regard sends a strong message: "We didn't care enough about you to get ready for your arrival." Prearrival phone calls and/or materials are part of preparing for new people, but it goes beyond that. Key people in the organization, including receptionists and the new hire's managers and colleagues, should be well aware of their impending arrival and have plans in place to help them get the best start, including as related to the points below. Family member employees can also be notified, to help offer a personal welcome. By the same token, it is also important for people to know whether the new employee is a family member, as discussed in the "Lisa's Secret" Box.

- *Have they been assigned a workspace?* The workspace assigned should make sense for the employee (such as a location within their division and/or near colleagues with whom they will collaborate regularly) and be conducive to greater motivation and performance (by addressing basic human needs such as space and light).

- *Have they been assigned a buddy or other source of early support?* A buddy or other support resource goes a long way to making a new person feel welcome. A dedicated individual/group can familiarize your new hires with the organization (from practical tips on workplace process to the inculcation of values and culture) and provide company for them at lunch, tours, and other activities.

- *Does the business know much about the employee?* As mentioned earlier, we see onboarding as a two-way integration, in which new employees and the organization become familiar with each other, adapting as needed. So it is important for the business to learn more about the employee than what they may present on their résumé or paperwork, even before the first day: What are their interests outside work? What work space accommodations might they need (not all needs in this domain are obvious)? Even what name they prefer to be addressed by is important to know before they start. Kwik Trip asks new hires about their hobbies, favorite foods, and how they like to be rewarded, in part to tailor rewards around these preferences.

- *Is there a comprehensive onboarding plan in place?* All of the items above and the others we discuss later in this chapter should be part of a systematic onboarding plan for new employees. In this area, as in most others we discuss, if you fail to plan, you are effectively planning to fail. Investing resources in comprehensive onboarding will pay off many times on multiple dimensions.

The table on page 115 summarizes our tips for establishing great first impressions and avoiding not-so-great ones through onboarding practices.

We want to highlight the importance of preparing family employees for working at the company, well before their first day. All of the points above relate to both family and nonfamily employees, but new *family* employees require an additional layer of preparation to ensure their behavior—and the organization's in relation to them—sends the right message to the broader firm. Even when a family desires that

Establishing GREAT First Impressions

Before and During First Days

- Identify and share with team desired outcomes for onboarding the new employee in his/her first 90 days
- Share company history/values and/or samples/examples of company products/services in advance
- Ensure people know the new employee is coming
- Assign a buddy before new employee arrives
- Send employee handbook, org chart, vision, mission, and other documents in advance
- Choreograph the first day(s) to ensure the new employee gets to know the people with whom he/she will be working (internal and external), including any owning family members who work in the business
- Host prearranged lunch for first day (include their favorite food)
- Ensure care and cleanliness of office space
- Host welcome reception with many participants
- Introduce new person to everyone by walking around
- Plan at least one activity (tour, introduction to area of business, etc.) for each day of the first week

its members should receive no special treatment, individuals who are both family members and employees will inevitably be looked at differently and often treated differently than their nonfamily coworkers. They also carry the responsibility of following the business's values and culture to a greater extent than others do. As such, new family employees can benefit from advice regarding how to conduct themselves from day one as family representatives within the business. At the core is exercising good judgment across settings and situations. This can extend to being careful regarding the "flaunting" of wealth (not many entry-level employees drive Porsches or bring Prada bags to work at most companies) or acting entitled in any way (from parking spaces to special projects, as discussed earlier). It can also apply to communication. Nonfamily employees may share information concerning their perceptions of the business and/or colleagues with family employees—this feedback can be positive but may be negative as well. It is important for the family to discuss how they want to deal with this information and to prepare family employees to effectively respond to others when it occurs. Similarly, family employees are privy to inside information that others may not know (such as owner and/or executive decisions). So family employees need to understand when and how to share information—about the family, the business, or their colleagues—across the territories they occupy, and when to choose silence. There are no hard and fast rules as to what should or should not be shared, but we will offer this guidance: only share information when absolutely certain it is okay to do so. If you are uncertain at all, it is best to keep it private. We have seen much more damage from a shared comment that should have been kept confidential than from a piece of information that was withheld unnecessarily.

Lisa's "Secret"

When third-generation cousin Lisa joined her family's consumer goods firm, she was surprised when her new colleagues asked how she knew about the job. No one had informed the group that Lisa was a member of the owning family, and this led to initial awkwardness for all parties. When a new family employee is joining the business, it is best to take a clear but casual approach, making sure her group knows her background before she arrives, while communicating (in words and actions) that she is to be treated like any other employee. There are, of course, cases in which family employees, especially those with different last names and/ or who work in more remote locations, appreciate the ability to "fly below the radar," at least initially. Such decisions may be made on a case-by-case basis, but we suggest erring on the side of sharing family member status information, for fairness and to avoid any subsequent tensions.

In general, the best overall guideline to follow is to use good judgment, care, and awareness in conducting oneself, ideally learning from those who have been there before. Similarly, the firm should take great pains to avoid what could be perceived as unfair preferential treatment of family employees, as in our opening scenario here. When such treatment is institutionalized, it hurts morale, motivation, and performance, risking the business's survival. The HR function can be particularly helpful in developing guidelines to inform family employee behavior. The family, ideally, will also develop such policies through family meetings and discussions. The result can even be a family employee training module that helps new employees understand how to conduct themselves optimally as they integrate into the business. All of this can be an important component of onboarding.

The First Day

An employee's first day sets the stage for all of the others they will have at your firm. So it is important for it to be an empowering rather than demoralizing experience. We have found the items below to be especially enriching first-day components.

- *Meet-and-greet activity:* Some kind of dedicated event to introduce new employees to the organization and their closer colleagues is ideal. For a smaller firm (say, under 50–100 people total), this may take the form of an all-employee breakfast—quarterly or monthly should be sufficient, depending on the number of new hires during such periods. At larger firms, it might be a divisional or group get-together, such as the one discussed in our opening example. It could also be an after-work activity (such as a happy hour), but those can be hit-or-miss in terms of attendance, and an experience that takes place earlier in the day is often best. As discussed in more detail below, the owning family may participate in these events as well.
- *Buddy:* As mentioned earlier, assigning a buddy for the first day or week is a great way to help new hires feel supported. Buddies should be chosen for their familiarity with the new person's area/work (a close colleague, for example) and their interpersonal skills—do they make others feel welcome? A good buddy not only provides practical information but also embodies the firm's values and culture, serving as an early role model.
- *Orientation:* Effective orientation events (whether on the first day or during the first week) include a mix of procedural information (such as where/how to get an employee badge, how to fill out payroll-related paperwork, and computer/tech-related tasks) and a focus on the business's history, culture, and values. Many orientations that we have seen include a tour of the company (both its main facilities and administrative areas, such as where to make photocopies and/or get office supplies),

along with video material related to the family's and business's history. It is especially valuable to have family members speak in person at the orientation about the firm's values and culture, ideally using their own experience as illustration. At a midsized retail firm we know, the founder makes it a point to meet briefly with all new employees, at any level, to get to know them personally and pass along his take on the company's values. This sends a clear message that the owning family cares about new employees and is accessible to them. And family representatives can be involved in welcoming and educating new employees even if they are not working in the business, whether through in-person interaction, videos, or some other form. Again, this sends a clear message that the owners care and are involved.

- *One-on-one/Team meeting:* Having the new employee meet one-on-one with their manager or with their broader team can set the stage for task-related and personal interaction. Emphasizing informality in such meetings on the first day can help the new employee ease into their new role and network, while helping the existing team get to know the new member better.

Kwik Trip makes its first day of onboarding all about the firm's culture, mission, and values. "We don't flood new people with policies and benefit-related information on their first day," says John McHugh, the firm's Manager of Corporate Communication and Leadership Development. Instead, Kwik Trip employees who have just arrived, hear motivational stories about how people at the firm live its mission and values. For example, new employees were recently told about an 18-year-old Kwik Trip cashier who gave his socks to a teenager (who had previously been in trouble for shoplifting from the store) when he saw the young man outside the store without socks on a cold day. The youth's parents wrote a glowing letter of compliment to the store manager. "The story shows how mission driven we are," McHugh says, "and we want to emphasize our mission right from the start."

Beyond the specific components presented above, it is important to develop strong organizational awareness of the need to support new people thoughtfully from the very beginning. Are your established employees willing to go out of the way to help their new colleagues, even if it is not part of their official responsibilities? If not, how can you encourage this behavior throughout your company? Do you think new employees would feel comfortable asking for help with their responsibilities and/or procedural matters? The way new people are treated speaks volumes about your firm's culture, so answers to these questions may illuminate deeper issues within the organization and guide you to begin tackling them on multiple levels.

It is best if a family employee's first day looks like that of any other employee, with the same combination of components as above. Established family employees sometimes wonder whether they should spend time with new family employees, because they worry that this may result in some perception of "special" status for the new employee. We see no problem with this, as long as everyone follows the overarching guideline of not institutionalizing special privileges for family members, whether parking spaces, projects, or office space. Such entitlements and/or expectations serve no one. However, some recognition of family status is natural and indeed expected, and this can be determined in part by the company's culture and in part by the new employee's needs/preferences. Many families make sure that entering family employees are thoroughly knowledgeable about any family policies, guidelines, or codes of conduct so that they can be thoroughly supportive of them.

The First Week

A new employee's first week at the business should build carefully on their prearrival and first-day experience. This is the time when they are acclimating more deeply not only to their new role and responsibilities but also to the culture and values of the business and the family that owns it. Thus we see an effective first week as representing a combination of ongoing overview and exposure, with several parties contributing to the integration of new employees.

Overview: The first week should include a continuing overview of the business and family, whether as part of formal training or more informal knowledge sharing. As discussed in greater depth in the "Development" chapter, during this time the new employee will familiarize themselves with their role, group, and division, in terms of both the tasks they will take on and the dynamics of the suborganizations to which they belong, as framed by the business's ongoing objectives. A manufacturing firm might take new employees on an in-depth tour of their facilities, so that they can get a sense of the bigger picture of operations, along with better clarity on their role within it. A management consulting firm would likely go over the frameworks and tools it uses for client engagements, along with expectations regarding team and client interactions. In both cases, the ideal approach involves a balance of actually doing the work and learning best practices by observing or being taught by established employees.

The first week is also a good time to help nonfamily employees understand some of the specific issues related to working for a family business. Some of this may be covered by orientation events that speak to structure, values, and culture, as discussed above, or a focus on "what makes us special" as a family business. Other elements may include how to appreciate and deal with family dynamics—and, of course, this is often relevant for family employees too! Topics covered could include "Family Business 101" components (including the strengths of family business versus others) and the distinctions among the three constituent groups: ownership, family, and business (discussed in the "Introduction" chapter), especially for employees completely new to a family business environment. Employees who have worked in both family and nonfamily business settings can be important contributors to such discussions/presentations.

Exposure: The overview component discussed above should expose new employees, including family and nonfamily members, to the business's mission, structure, processes, objectives, values, and culture. Here we focus on the *people* part of exposure, or the promotion of interactions among new hires and the different groups and individuals within the business. It is ideal for people to meet colleagues from across groups, levels, and divisions, to promote organization-wide collaboration and more innovative thinking. It is especially important to ensure interaction among family and nonfamily employees, again to send a clear message regarding impartial treatment of all employees. Interaction may take place formally, through dedicated group lunches or other types of events, or informally, whether through happy hours or just in the hallways of firms with cultures that promote open atmospheres.

In the case of family employees, broad exposure is important. We have observed that family members working in businesses with a large group of family employees often tend to keep their interactions within the family, given that they are already familiar with one another. In some cases they even stick with their closer relatives, rather than mingling with more distant family members and other employees. This behavior creates an "us versus them" mentality that benefits no one. So it is important to make sure family employees have a large set of interactions, especially in their early weeks.

Remember: onboarding is not a one-way street; it is important for the business also to understand and communicate what is expected of new employees at key milestones: such as 30, 60, and 90 days after being hired. Setting clear goals, outputs, and deliverables for each new employee early and "exposing" them to these through careful communication is critical, as it helps both the business and employee set (and meet) expectations.

Integration support: Integration of new employees is a team effort ideally involving the employee themselves, their supervisor and team, as well as any assigned buddy (as described earlier), and HR. For example, while the supervisor, team, and buddy can help familiarize the employee with role-related responsibilities and the internal social network, someone from HR can support this with procedural and cultural knowledge. In fact, HR staff in family businesses will ideally have specific training to understand the dynamics associated with family enterprise, allowing them to help new employees navigate the related complexity. For new leaders, an outside board member can be a particularly helpful mentor, whether on a formal or informal basis.

It often works well to assign a family member as a buddy or mentor for a new family employee, in part to help the new hire understand the tricky terrain a family member must navigate while working for the business, as mentioned earlier. Similarly, a buddy may end up being a short-term source of support or be transformed into a longer-term mentor (or someone else may end up in a formal or informal mentor role). In all cases, the hope is that after the end of any formal buddy/mentorship period, the individual will continue to serve as an important resource and role model for the new employee.

First 90 Days—and Beyond

Many firms make the mistake of seeing onboarding as a very time-limited process, and that employees are effectively "on board" after their first week or two. In reality, new hires experience ongoing adjustment to the organization, and vice versa, over their first months and even years at the company. In fact, organizational researcher Michael Watkins has shown that a new employee *consumes* value from the business for their first three months, only after which they begin *adding* value. In fact, the break-even point—at which the new employee adds more value than they consume—comes only after 6.2 months, on average.[6] In our experience, this holds true for family firms.

A thoughtful, strategic onboarding process takes this fact into account by building in key elements well after new employees' first week or even month. A primary component we recommend for ongoing onboarding is *check-ins*. Regular check-ins ensure that new employees are gaining value from the onboarding process and provide your organization feedback to improve onboarding elements. They can be conducted by the employee's direct supervisor, by HR, or alternatively by each. We recommend weekly check-ins for the first month, then biweekly for the second and third months, with modification as needed for a given person or role. Check-ins can be brief formal surveys assessing employees' onboarding experience, informal conversations (such as with their buddy, mentor, or HR contact), or some combination. The important thing is to make clear to new employees that you value their feedback and will work hard to improve their experience—and that of future new hires. The check-in is also a time to review and reward employee performance and plan for future development, as discussed at length in the "Development" chapter. For example, Kwik Trip does a full performance appraisal based on expected core competencies at the 90-day mark. The reviews are expected to generate three specific goals for each employee (such as being more empathetic), even if they are performing at a high level, as part of a focus on continual improvement.

This general formula for check-ins extends to the time period when employees are not so new—the first-year check-in is an important means of assessing an employee's progress as well as what the business can do better to integrate new people in the future. This check-in is also an important time to review/reward performance and to set a development plan. We recommend some kind of one-year celebration—even an informal team lunch is a nice way to mark this important milestone. As always, determine what works best for your business with regard to the check-in process, as part of a general philosophy of *constant evolution*.

Second, we advocate a *careful approach to onboarding leaders*. Sometimes this means longer formal onboarding for new leaders. Kwik Trip, for example, has a four-week onboarding program for new store leaders, and much shorter programs for other roles such as those in the production facility. For leadership roles, the onboarding process can progress through several stages: what is working, as far as task-related and management practices, and should be kept in place; what is not working and should be eliminated; what improvements need to be made; and what responsibilities and/or activities should be added for the leader. One part of this approach can be a New Manager Integration Exercise, as discussed further in the box below. Formal coaching, as part of a more comprehensive plan, can address these areas as needed (especially those with steeper learning curves) and enhance performance. The entire approach to onboarding new leaders is best captured by developing a comprehensive plan including role expectations, goals, and check-ins. In fact, a study by Harvard researchers shows that only companies with a detailed plan were able to assimilate new leaders effectively.[7] So plan carefully around onboarding new leaders, and remember to check in frequently, rather than assuming that people, even leaders, will always speak up when they need something or find that things are not working effectively.

New Manager Integration Exercise

We advocate this exercise to "jump-start" team dynamics with a new manager. The 2-to-4-hour exercise can be part of a new manager's onboarding, and can take place early in their tenure, with flexibility around timing. The general process involves having a facilitator work with the new manager and team:

- First, the facilitator and manager welcome the team and explain the process.

- Then, the manager leaves the room while the facilitator goes over potential questions the team can ask the manager (What do you want to know about the manager? What concerns do you have regarding the new manager? What does the manager need to know about you?) And the facilitator also solicits other questions. (Based on your early experiences in the job, do you have any feedback? What's working well? What can be improved?) This could be about any aspect of the employee's experience.
- Then, the facilitator and the manager meet one-on-one to discuss the questions and the manager's response.
- Finally, the entire group reconvenes and the manager answers the questions, along with setting a follow-up plan.

Pitfalls

Here we point out some of the most common pitfalls we have seen with onboarding.

- *Not taking onboarding seriously:* The biggest issue we have observed is a failure to take onboarding seriously. Some firms do not see the value in crafting a specific program to integrate new hires. Some managers believe that "people will just show up and work," especially if their firm has a more casual, do-it-yourself culture. However, these family businesses are missing an important opportunity to inspire and motivate people by showing them from the start of their tenure the firm's value and that the business cares about its employees. Onboarding helps ground new employees in key knowledge and networks, ensuring they deliver their best performance. A failure to take it seriously can make your firm lose the person and their performance before they even begin their role in earnest.
- *Failing to take an organization-wide approach to onboarding:* Onboarding should be an "all-play," one that involves a wide range of people and groups in the organization. That relates to those who plan the onboarding process—which should include HR and other areas—and those who participate in its execution, including family (employees and outside members) and

nonfamily peers. It is important to get senior leaders as involved in onboarding as possible, as well, to show management's commitment to integrating new people. And for the onboarding of new family employees, especially successor candidates, it is important for multiple generations to be involved, including the incoming and outgoing ones. Relegating onboarding to the HR department or function alone will fail to take advantage of the other rich resources across the business. In short, strive for a more integrative approach to transitioning new hires into the business.

- *Taking a one-size-fits-all approach:* It is critical to find the specific onboarding approach that works for you—one that is aligned with the culture of your organization. In some cases, for example, highlighting the family-owned aspect of the business will help integrate new employees more seamlessly, while in others it might not. We present many ideas and guidelines here, but that does not mean we want you to use *all* of them in a specific, prescriptive way. Take the ones that you believe will work for your enterprise and adapt them as needed, learning as you go.

Things to Remember: An Onboarding Checklist

We hope we have made clear the importance of onboarding for every new employee. The start counts, and we recommend an integrative, two-way process to derive the greatest benefits for employees and the business alike. The onboarding checklist (Table 6.1) summarizes the many specific tips we presented in this chapter.

Table 6.1   An onboarding checklist

Pre-First Day

- Meet with supervisor, buddy and team members to plan first 30 days for most effective internal and external integration
- Clarify roles and responsibilities for onboarding between HR, direct supervisor, coworkers, etc.
- Send Welcome Package
  - Welcome letter from CEO (or direct supervisor
  - Welcome and introduction letter from family
  - FB Vision, Mission, and Values
  - FB history
  - Organization chart
  - Sample products (if applicable)
- Notify company employees and family of new hire
- Organize new employee set-up (business cards, workspace, employee badge, e-mail address, intranet logon ID/password, inclusion on e-mail distribution lists, etc.)
- Establish a buddy for new hire
- Plan for Day 1 meetings, tours, and lunch
- For family employees, clarify any additional plans such as review of family employment guidelines, assignment of family mentor, and the like

First Day

- Send reminder to staff about new hire start
- Introduce new hire to all staff by walking around
- Meet and greet with buddy
- Tour of office facilities and work space
- Take new employee/leaders to lunch (buddy and/or manager and/or team)
- Complete HR paperwork
- Review employee handbook

First Week

- Tour other facilities (e.g., manufacturing plant, if applicable)
- Meet with family members and/or mentor (if applicable)
- Conduct company orientation session (ideally first day, but at least by first week) (HR)
  - Review FB company background and history
  - Discuss differences between FB and non-FB (important so as not to make FB an undiscussable topic)
  - Deliver family business cultural integration session

Continued

Table 6.1   Continued

- Conduct Job/Functional Orientation to new role and responsibilities (boss/team)
- Review function, role, and responsibilities
- Review organizational systems, procedures, structures
- Meet with team (conduct New Manager Integration exercise, if applicable)
- Provide initial work assignment(s)

First 90 Days

- Conduct regular check-ins (frequency dependent on role, likely to be weekly or biweekly)
- Support, coach, and provide informal feedback to new employee/leader
- Reward and recognize value and contributions
- Obtain feedback from new employee/leader
- Introduce new employee to others via company newsletter, website news feed, etc.
- 90-day performance review (see below)

6 Months

- 120-day performance review

Annual Check-in

- Reward and recognize value and contributions
- Annual performance review and development plan
- One-year celebration

7

Development

Joseph Phelps Vineyards, based in Napa Valley, California, is well known for its wines, including the award-winning Insignia Bordeaux-style blend. A fully integrated wine company, the third-generation family business owns 450 acres of vines and sells about 65,000 cases of wine annually. Along with growing and processing grapes, the company fosters a different kind of growth: the development of its employees, a 100-strong workforce that now includes third-generation family members. But that emphasis on development was not always in place. "The company didn't put much thought into development, especially for family employees, when I joined in the late '90s," recalls Bill Phelps, the founder's son and current CEO, who entered the firm as only the second family employee, after two decades working as an attorney.

Since then, the business has made development a priority. For example, the full-time HR director has worked with the company's leadership and the board members to create a structured development system to promote the growth of family and nonfamily employees alike. This has been particularly important for Will Phelps and Elizabeth Neuman, third-generation cousins now working in the business.

As we will discuss throughout this chapter, elements of a strong development system—the next component of the HR lifecycle—include means of assessing performance and capability gaps, outcomes based on that performance review, a specific development plan, and a "mini-cycle" of learning and coaching/feedback. Joseph Phelps Vineyards exemplifies these components, using them to help Will, Elizabeth, and other employees and owners develop their skills with a fair-minded performance review system, multiple ownership development efforts, and learning opportunities including a project-based learning program and mentorship from independent directors on the board.

"It's vital for us to get development right," Bill says.

*   *   *

Bill Phelps is absolutely right: Development is a critical component of family business performance. We believe that an optimal approach to development in the family business involves creating a culture of continuous learning and a mind-set of constant evolution. Constant evolution takes place on multiple dimensions, for individual employees and for the business as a whole. Rather than reflecting a narrow set of practices or policies, employee development is ideally reflected in an ongoing, iterative cycle of assessment, learning, and coaching.

Before we dive into specifics, let us think about *why* development is important to family firms in the first place. The human factor in any company is essential. Everything that makes up your firm—machinery, facilities, processes, and other elements—is replicable, with one exception: your people. Finding ways to help your people develop to the full extent of their abilities is an investment worth making. As evidence, firms that excel at developing their talent have been found to generate 15 percent greater returns than their peers.[1]

But today, due to multiple converging trends including an aging population base, the high departure rate of employees, and the shifting expectations of the Millennial cohort, it can be harder than ever to find, keep, and replace good people. For many employees, the decision to exit is based on a lack of engagement with their jobs and the company. Frequently, there is a perception of inadequate opportunities for individual growth and development, and a hope that greater opportunities for development exist elsewhere. Also, workplaces are continuously changing and evolving, so it is essential to business performance that employees are also continuously growing and developing in their skills and abilities. It is no surprise that firms across sectors cite development as a critical issue in performance.

Taken together, these factors highlight the importance of managing people such that they grow in terms of capabilities and potential contributions, while engaging ever more deeply with the company and its mission. This is the domain of development, a critical process for getting the best out of your firm's most precious resource: your people. Development within a family business is especially important for the following reasons:

1. For any employee—family and nonfamily alike—the multiple overlapping systems of a family business can be tricky to navigate, and supporting the development of all employees' capabilities in this area will help them handle this tricky navigation more effectively.
2. For family employees specifically, any investment in their professional development has the added bonus of reaping rewards for the family as well, on multiple dimensions, from economic to professional to psychological.
3. Development can be an even more essential factor for family businesses because of their tendency toward insularity. Due to past success, family businesses can sometimes have a propensity to stick to "our way of doing things." They may be wary of outside input, including fresh ideas regarding how best to foster growth in employees.[2]
4. Family firms face the additional challenge of managing the performance and development of *family* employees in as an objective and effective a way as possible—a complexity not present in nonfamily firms.

In addition, the benefits of good development for any family business include

- getting the highest return on the human capital—both family and nonfamily—within your firm by boosting employee engagement, morale, and satisfaction;
- fostering a healthy relationship between family and nonfamily employees by building knowledge and understanding of family business dynamics and particularities;
- achieving top-notch results and competitive advantages generated by maximizing the resources within the family, as well as developing a highly capable and continuously improving workforce;
- developing leadership skill and capacity within the family and the business;

- facilitating effective succession planning at the ownership and management levels by creating a strong "bench" of motivated, long-term performers;
- reflecting and reinforcing a culture of learning, excellence, and constant evolution;
- providing real, meaningful feedback to people, which can be a very difficult process for both family and nonfamily employees because of the "family" atmosphere of the business; and
- creating a more transparent atmosphere in which family employees become more comfortable mentoring one another as needed (for succession, for example) and sharing development-related feedback

A systematic approach to development, fueled by effective HR practices, can ensure your family firm benefits from this essential element.

Development as a Continuous Cycle of Assessment, Learning, and Coaching

Standardized training, performance reviews, and promotions—while all of these are important to employee development, we believe the concept of development should stretch well past individual components. An ideal development system will reflect a continuous process of learning and growth that helps people regularly increase the breadth and depth of their engagement and contributions to the firm.

As such, development in your family business will ideally be a *fluid and dynamic* process, rather than a static and overly standardized one. That means building a development system based on multiple principles:

- *Mutual benefit:* Development is in the best interest of the individual employee *and* the company, and both need to develop for ideal results.
- *Intentionality:* Development, like culture (discussed extensively in its own chapter), should be conscious and intentional. Effective development will not just happen organically. It

requires a purposeful approach with deliberately planned processes and structures.

- *Capability- and culture focused:* Optimal development will breed competence and interpersonal/leadership skills—our twin dimensions of capability, as discussed in earlier chapters—at both the individual and organizational levels. Competence and softer skills contribute directly to a firm's culture and environment, especially as related to how people are treated and expect to be treated. Development both reflects and shapes your firm's culture and environment, with a good development system promoting a people-oriented culture and vice-versa.
- *Understanding of and appreciation for family business features:* Development in the family firm must be designed with consideration of special challenges such as the assessment and coaching of family members, as suggested by the list of benefits presented earlier.

A strategic effort at creating a strong development system can help your firm evolve into a true "learning organization" with elements of mastery, shared vision, and learning at every level.[3] At a high level, an effective development system works to strengthen and transform the "inputs" (human capital) available within your organization into the "outputs" (leaders, motivated, competent, and engaged employees) depicted in Figure 7.1.

While there are many books on development approaches in business contexts, our focus is on what is particularly important or tricky for family firms seeking to improve development. In this context,

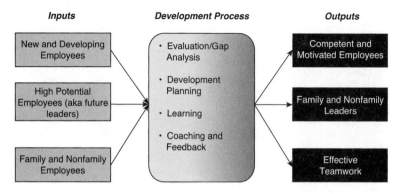

Figure 7.1   Inputs, process, and outputs of a good development system.

we want to encourage families and executives to seek the input and influence of the HR team with regard to development issues (or, for smaller firms, an outside HR consultant or view development from an HR lens), as this function is best equipped to help create, facilitate, and inform most development processes for family members.

Development System Components

An effective development system creates a cycle with mutually rein-forcing components as depicted in Figure 7.2. In this section we will present an overview of the overall development system, followed by in-depth discussion of each component.

As we emphasized earlier, the cycle reflects a dynamic process, with both formal and informal components. For example, while your business may have formal performance evaluations (or reviews, as many firms refer to them) at semiannual time points, informal feed-back is also an important component of development. This aspect of development is incorporated into Coaching and Feedback. The

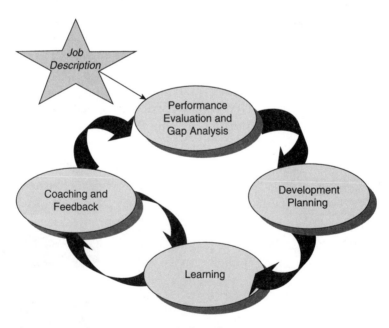

Figure 7.2   Development system cycle and components.

overall cycle, by definition, has an iterative component (that is what cycles do!), but note that there is also a "cycle within a cycle," as suggested by the loop between the Coaching and Feedback and Learning components in the visual. The idea is that development plans are usually not carried out in a linear, lockstep way. Instead, learning takes place best when it is accompanied by frequent coaching and feedback. This process promotes ongoing growth across both competence and interpersonal/leadership skills. With that in mind, let us consider each of the components of the development system.

Performance Evaluation and Gap Analysis

Evaluation of performance is a necessary but challenging process, especially when family employees are involved. Part of the challenge for many family firms is that they may not have clear *job descriptions or job-related goals* in place, and thus, they may lack clear criteria against which to evaluate performance. There may even be active resistance to pinning down the definition of a job, as was the case at one family firm we know, in which a second-generation member put off writing a job description for himself for months, for fear that it would lock him into a set of responsibilities he did not want. Such inertia may be understandable, but it is not beneficial. Resistance to specifying job responsibilities might also be related to an earlier stage of the business (e.g., start-up) in which everyone just "pitched in where needed." The loose, mutually supportive nature of early-stage family firms often needs to give way to a tighter, more performance-based approach. Many times, there is resistance to that evolution.

While we talk about the importance of the job description in other chapters—in "Recruiting," for example—we want to emphasize its importance here, as well. A thoughtful job description allows for meaningful conversations about a person's job performance. It also sets the stage for a discussion of where they should be headed. Even a basic job description fulfills this function. The formality/informality of job descriptions can vary widely between firms. Some firms have a strict approach that provides highly detailed descriptions for each position. Other firms (like high-performance-fabric manufacturer Gor-Tex) deliberately create highly elastic role definitions that continuously shift and evolve based on the need of the organization and the interests and abilities of the individual. See the "Job Description vs. Role Description" box for more on this issue.

Job Description vs. Role Description

Organizational development specialist Stephen Hurley, who consults with schools and other organizations, talks about the difference between a "job" and a "role."[4] He points out that jobs, as most of us think about them, tend to be *"discrete, defined,* and, in a sense, *limited."* That means they have clear boundaries related to time and space, and established criteria against which to evaluate performance. While jobs may be thought of as the *content,* including clear responsibilities and goals, a role is more like the *context,* providing a general notion of what someone is expected to do, but without the hard-and-fast definition a job might have. Roles thus tend to be more overarching, and associated with multiple jobs, but can be harder to define precisely.

Assuming some kind of job or role description is in place, it can help assess a person's readiness to take on the job, for example, a newly hired or recently promoted employee. It also provides a necessary basis for evaluating an individual's performance in the role to date. Again, there is a wide range of evaluation approaches on the formal-informal spectrum. Some firms have complex, comprehensive performance rating forms filled out by multiple parties, including an employee's supervisor, colleagues, and possibly even clients/customers/suppliers, with assessment of performance and development needs on multiple dimensions. Others may make do with a brief, unstructured conversation between an employee and manager about expectations and performance. In this section we will discuss performance evaluation that typically takes place as part of an annual or semiannual review, saving discussion of two specific approaches—one-on-one and 360-degree feedback—for the "Coaching and Feedback" section below.

There is no one "right answer" to what kind of evaluation process is best. Some firms use that fact to avoid or delay implementing an evaluation system in the first place. Many times, providing performance feedback, especially for family employees (particularly *underperforming* family employees), is felt to be an "undiscussable" topic. A systematic, professional approach to performance management is essential to business success, and the specific design of your system will depend largely on your firm's culture and objectives. A highly structured evaluation process does not imply an impersonal or rigid corporate culture, but rather a workplace that places strong emphasis on documented procedures and quantifiable results. Similarly, a more casual approach to evaluation does not mean that a firm is not serious about its performance or people, but more that its culture values informality and flexibility in its approaches, even regarding performance feedback. Whatever the firm's culture, we have found that it is essential to create an approach for assessing family employee performance. Some kind of *objective, standardized approach* is needed, rather than relying exclusively on informal observations and conversations. Evaluating members of the owning family can be awkward; therefore, a pre-established approach can help ensure that it actually takes place..

As far as what specific aspects of performance are evaluated, we emphasize assessment of *results*, but also advocate including aspects of the *process used to achieve results.* It is natural to focus on outcome elements like sales, revenue, growth, cost savings, customer conversion/acquisition, and other traditional outcome-linked performance measures, many of which are related to financial metrics. But failing to include interpersonal/process-related variables, including collaboration, communication, service, safety mindedness, and others, is a failure to acknowledge very importance elements of performance. Although less tangible, these factors support the values and culture of your firm that are well worth monitoring and evaluating as part of the performance management process. A performance evaluation system that speaks to process-related metrics reinforces a people-focused culture, as do measures of performance at the group/team and organizational level. Overall, an optimal performance management system makes clear the performance elements most valued by the firm, along with measuring these carefully and offering recognition when success has been achieved.

Below we present an example of a comprehensive performance evaluation form (Table 7.1).

Table 7.1   A performance evaluation form

Name:	Job Title:
Length in Current Position:	Reporting Manager:

Instructions

The Performance Feedback Process is a review of employees' performance over one full reporting period (fiscal year). Please complete the following:

- **Part A: Performance and Competency Goals**—Throughout the course of the year, review and update your performance- and competency-related goals. Please indicate the status of the goal during the Year-End Review (completed, in-progress, not started).
- **Part B:. Organizational Competencies**—Assess your own level of each competency.
- **Part C: Accomplishments and Development Areas**—Provide specific feedback about the employee's accomplishments and areas for development since the previous year's review.

Part A: Performance and Competency Goals

Define and enter your performance and competency goals at a high level using SMART criteria: **Specific, Measurable, Attainable, Realistic, and Time Bound.**

Performance Goals	Indicate Status

1: EXAMPLE: Increase annual sales by 15%
  • Meet and exceed objectives outlined in the scorecard quarterly
  • Review strategy in Q2 and adjust plan to reach 15% target	

2: EXAMPLE: Implement new accounting system in remote offices by Q3 • Develop implementation plan and strategy by Q1	

Competency Goals	Status
1: EXAMPLE: Obtain CMA certification in Q2	
2: EXAMPLE: Strengthen management skills capability by completing XYZ's Mgmt Fundamentals program by Q4	

continued

Table 7.1 Continued

Part B: XYZ Organizational Competencies

Both the manager and employee complete an assessment of the employee and compare results.

	Developing	Improvement Needed	Meets Expectations	Exceeds Expectations	Exceptional
Ranking Definitions	Performance has met most job accountabilities and objectives throughout the reporting period. Employee is developing in a new role and solid performance is expected in the next reporting period,	Performance has not met job accountabilities and objectives throughout the reporting period. Plans need to be and/or are in place toward ensuring immediate and sustained improvements.	Performance has successfully met job accountabilities and objectives throughout the reporting period.	Performance has met and often/ frequently exceeded job accountabilities and objectives throughout the reporting period.	Performance has clearly and consistently exceeded job accountabilities and objectives throughout the reporting period. Contribution is recognized as outstanding.
Target Distribution	0–5%	1–10%	50%	30%	10%

Competency	Self Assessment	Manager Assessment	Comments
Demonstrates problem solving/critical thinking skills • Thinks analytically and conceptually, questioning and challenging the status quo to identify issues…			Employee: Manager:
Communicates effectively • Listens well and encourages open exchange of information and ideas using appropriate media			Employee: Manager:

continued

Table 7.1   Continued

Part C: Accomplishments and Development Areas

Accomplishments: Where does my performance exceed expectations?
Comments by Employee:
Comments by Manager:
Development Areas: Where is further improvement required?
Comments by Employee:
Comments by Manager:

Personal Development Plan

Review and update your career and professional development goals.

What are my short-term (1–3 years) professional growth and career aspirations? What do I want to achieve or master in my role?

Short-term (1–3 years)

What are my long-term (3–5 years) professional growth and career aspirations? What is it that I would like to create or achieve in 3–5 years?

What knowledge, skills, or abilities do I need to enhance in order to achieve my short-term and long-term goals?

What actions do I need to take in order to obtain these goals?

An ideal performance evaluation process will also make clear *gaps related to both competence and interpersonal skills*. Specifically, the discussion can illuminate where a given person needs to develop additional capabilities to perform their current or future role. Competence-related gaps are those concerning technical (such as finance, engineering, and others) or general skills (such as presentation capabilities) required for success in the job. The box below presents tips for analyzing performance effectively within family business.

Tips for an Effective Performance Feedback Process within Family Businesses

- Start the process with mutually understood expectations that are clearly articulated from the beginning (based on job description, performance criteria, etc.).
- Clarify who will participate in the feedback process including family and nonfamily members. Get feedback from multiple sources.
- Commit to open and honest communication.
- Maintain strict confidentiality. Performance is a private matter.
- Be sure the process positively impacts the individual. Focus on the positive as well as areas for improvement.
- Utilize an objective tool for measuring performance so that it does not feel like a criticism coming from a parent, sibling or other family member.
- Focus the process on determining what a person is really good at doing and align their skills and interests with business needs

Outcomes

As mentioned above, a good performance management system makes clear the performance elements that matter most, measures these, and rewards them. Rewards, in the form of financial compensation, promotion, benefits/perks, and recognition, represent one outcome that emerges from performance evaluation.[5] Negative outcomes can include various forms of demotion (in terms of title or salary), and, of course, termination. We offer several guiding principles to help you think about the role of outcomes in your firm's development system.

- *Ensure your rewards reflect the right results.* It seems obvious that rewards should reflect results, but this can be a tricky area in family firms. It is tempting, for example, to use more elastic definitions of results for family employees. However, that can create a dangerous precedent and a non-merit-focused environment that hampers collective performance. Similarly, use of rewards will communicate which results are most valued, whether they be revenues, profitability, growth, or more process-focused measures such as collaboration. One of the authors of this book comes from a family business that shifted its compensation of sales managers from sales based to collections based, as the business had been struggling to collect payments from several large customers, which resulted in diminishing cash flow. Improvement came almost overnight as employees strengthened their focus on collecting overdue payments.

- *Understand that outcomes symbolize culture.* Again it is no surprise that the nature of outcomes—and their basis—in your firm will reflect its culture and values. If financially related results are rewarded above other results, the focus of employee performance will be on financials. As we mentioned above, an emphasis on rewarding nontraditional outcomes (such as innovation) or processes (such as collaboration) can go a long way toward supporting a desired culture. This may seem obvious, but it is important to use outcomes that effectively reflect the culture you wish to reinforce.

- *Separate business and family.* While family and business are naturally intertwined in family firms, it is important to separate these with regard to outcomes. As mentioned above, overpaying family employees can be a slippery slope with widespread negative impact. Similar caution must be exercised around promotions and demotions. Question: How do you know when a family employee is ready for promotion, demotion, or termination? Answer: If they meet (or do not meet) the criteria that any nonfamily employee would have to meet for these outcomes. The presence of a baseline culture of meritocracy will make such decisions easier for everyone, as will a system of documenting performance evaluation and development plans. Moreover, recognition of the dangers of unduly favoring family can help motivate more objective approaches. Retention or promotion of a poorly performing family employee sends an undesirable message to everyone in the firm—"performance is much less important than family status"—and can demotivate others. At the same time, part of the value that family employees bring is their ability to convey the family's continuing commitment to the firm, so that can be legitimately considered in their performance assessment Merely adequate performance from some family employees may be sufficient to serve that goal.

Joseph Phelps Vineyards' practices reflect these principles well, especially the idea of treating family and nonfamily employees similarly, as much as possible. Compensation-related outcomes are based on a performance review system developed by the HR director. Salaries, raises, and bonuses are all constructed on current market rates. Promotions are also determined by measuring performance against explicit expectations and criteria. "Performance management is essentially the same for family and nonfamily," said second-generation CEO Bill Phelps. "There's no exception for being a family member," his son Will added, but then clarified that "if two people are exactly equally qualified, we might favor the family member, given our long-term perspective and goals, but the decision would be made carefully by managers with input from our independent board members."

Along with generating logical outcomes, a comprehensive performance evaluation points to any issues that should be addressed through careful development planning, which is our next topic.

Development Planning

Development planning serves a simple but specific purpose: getting an employee to a point at which they are performing optimally. As mentioned above, this often entails addressing specific gaps, whether related to competence, soft skills, or a combination. But development planning is about more than addressing gaps—it is about helping the individual grow and increase their abilities to deliver at their highest level of performance. Development planning is important for employees at all levels, but we want to call attention to several groups in particular.

Future Owners: Current or future family owners will benefit from gaining competency in what we call "ownership skills." In fact, next-generation owners might consider creating a development plan specifically focused on becoming knowledgeable, prepared, owners, as illustrated in our learning model, presented later in this chapter. This plan might include developing an understanding of the industry and the history of family ownership, learning the terms of the firm's buy-sell agreement, observing board meetings, and participating in conferences to learn from members of other high-functioning family firms. For example, one of us comes from a family in the agricultural business in which family owners participate in presentations from leading companies in agriculture on topics such as seed traits, performance, and technologies to help us understand our business and the industry in which it functions. For family members working in the business who wish to also develop as future owners, we recommend applying an "80/20" approach. Family members would ideally plan to spend about 80 percent of their time on job-related tasks and 20 percent on developing these ownership skills. An ideal development plan will reflect this proportion.

At the Joseph Phelps Vineyards, the firm developed an internship opportunity that started informally but became a structured summer program for family members in high school and college. Most of the third-generation family members went through the program, gaining exposure to areas that included the vineyard, cellar, hospitality, and office assistance work. Other ownership development activities have included attendance at family and annual shareholder meetings (where they participate in presentations about the business's history, performance, and ownership structure, among other topics) and family business seminars. Elizabeth Neuman, the first member of the third generation to join the business, said, "These have been important ways to pass on our family's history and knowledge." Second-generation CEO Bill Phelps said, "Even if they don't work in the business, this helps develop them as owners and ambassadors of the company."

Successors: Not surprisingly, development planning is critical for the rising generation of family (and nonfamily) leaders in the business. Family successors will need to gain required job-related skills—in the domains of both competence and interpersonal/leadership capabilities. Multiple books advise comprehensively on managing succession "successfully" in family business.[6] Family business expert John L. Ward proposes a specific development timeline to consider for successor development, as suggested by Table 7.2.[7]

This chart is useful for helping family businesses consider how to engage and develop the next generation from the early stages of life. On the surface this concept may seem extensive, but when you

Table 7.2 A development timeline for successors

Successor's Role	Child growing up at home:	Young adult: learning outside the family business	Professional manager: mentored within the business	Successor: designated as heir; mentored by senior executive or board members	Leader: CEO or member of the senior management team	Chairperson: leads the board and supports the CEO
Age	0–18	18–28	25–35	30–40	35–65	55–70
Developmental Goals	Positive attitude toward the business, basic education, skill development, and positive work habits	Higher education: develop self-confidence and organizational skills and begin career exploration	Functional expertise and planning, coaching, decision-making, and problem-solving skills	General management and profit center responsibility	Executive development: personal growth, self-awareness, and continuing education	Life planning: exploring other interests and opportunities

Note: That the ages in the table are provided as guidelines rather than recommendations.

consider the intention is for the next generation to start out with a positive, healthy view of the family business, including understanding how it contributes to the welfare of the family, it is important to start as early as possible. There is a lot of work to be done to prepare the next generation—whether it is for leadership and management or just ownership!

Our colleague Stephen Miller has done extensive research on approaches to developing next-generation family business leaders, as highlighted in the "Developing Next-Generation Leaders" Box.

Developing Next-Generation Leaders

Family business researcher and consultant Stephen Miller studied next-generation leadership in family firms and found that the following circumstances and steps resulted in development of more effective, satisfied successors:[8]

- a family climate characterized by open communication, shared values and norms
- a senior generation that attends to the welfare and needs of the younger generation, rather than wielding unquestioned authority
- careful attention to governance systems, including regular family meetings aimed at fostering communication, promoting shared values, and creating leadership opportunities
- the provision of next-generation leaders with job assignments characterized by genuine responsibility, accountability, and risk
- accurate feedback on performance, often from trusted nonfamily business leaders

Third-generation members Will and Elizabeth of Joseph Phelps Vineyards have benefited from a focus on their development as potential successors of the family wine business. With specific roles in the firm already, they fall into the early stage of the Professional Manager column of the table above. As Elizabeth noted, "It's important to think about development, not just succession, very early, and with the big picture in mind, with multiple paths and opportunities for development." Her uncle (and Will's father) and second-generation CEO Bill Phelps, said, "We want them involved in specific benchmarking and mentoring programs, with specific objectives to groom them for larger future roles." In line with this, the business adopted a professional development program—designed with the board's help—in late 2014, with several components aimed specifically at Elizabeth's and Will's development. The program includes exposure to a broad range of sales and marketing opportunities and high-profile projects outside these domains, as discussed more in the "Learning" section below. "As future leaders of the company, we are in a unique situation and will benefit from unique learning experiences," Will said.

Nonfamily executives: It is smart to pay special attention to the development needs of nonfamily executives, especially around their understanding of family business issues. A good development plan for professionals in this group might include training related to family business issues (such as leadership/governance seminars provided by university-based family business centers, as discussed in the "Learning" section below) and mentorship from family executives and independent directors on the family business board (or potentially even from family leaders outside the business).

Jeff Vincent, the nonfamily CEO and President of Laird Norton Company since 2001, offers a few key "words of wisdom" for other nonfamily executives:

- The family's legacy is central to any major decision.
- The time horizon in family businesses is longer than in nonfamily businesses (i.e., think about the *next* generation).
- The focus should be on values.
- Decisions are more personal in a family business (i.e., decisions are not so wrenching in a nonfamily business).
- You should communicate, communicate, communicate!
- As a nonfamily executive, you are responsible for something special, something you cannot buy—fundamentally, it is a group of people.

Though not necessarily part of a development plan, clear communication regarding the potential for their advancement—including whether there is a glass ceiling in place—can benefit nonfamily executives, as well. All of this can help keep nonfamily executives motivated while building their capacity for dealing with family business issues, dynamics, and politics.[9] Again, Joseph Phelps Vineyards has taken clear steps to develop senior nonfamily managers. "We need to support them as they work with family and nonfamily employees and help them understand some of the distinctions in the development needs of each," said CEO Bill Phelps.

Learning

Because learning is a key goal for all stakeholders within the firm, development should take place at the individual, team, and organizational levels on both the family and business sides, as suggested by Figure 7.3.

- *Individual level*: Learning at the individual level on the *business side* is focused on building capability and capacity in functional skills such as operations, finance, marketing, and sales, as well as overall personal skills such as judgment, initiative, and so on; whereas, learning at the individual level on the *family side* involves understanding who you are (i.e., style, preferences, strengths) in relation to those in your family (as well as others) and learning how to manage yourself in the context of a family

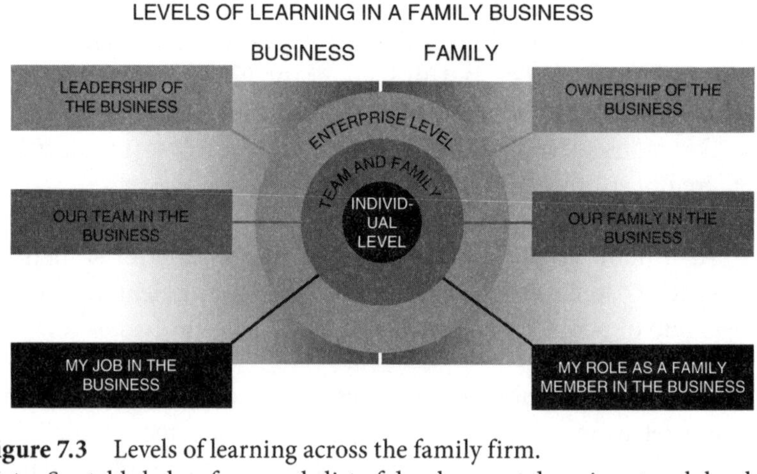

Figure 7.3 Levels of learning across the family firm.
Note: See table below for sample list of development domains at each level.

business (e.g., setting boundaries, responding to criticism such as nepotism or entitlement).

- *Team level*: Learning at the team level on the *business side* consists of all things related to being part of a high-performing team within the overall context of the business history, industry, and markets; whereas, learning at the team level on the *family side* involves understanding the family's history includinginfluential family members, having the ability to work together inside and outside of the business, and so on.
- *Organizational level*: Learning at the organizational level on the *business side* entails learning to lead with values, managing change and growth, and driving forward by using strategy, process improvement, and the like. Learning at this level on the *family side* consists of understanding how to be an effective owner and governor of a family business, including letting go, stewarding the business, building community, and so on.

Table 7.3 provides a summary of the levels of learning. It is not meant to be prescriptive but rather representative of the type of learning that is helpful in a family enterprise.

In this context, the core focus of any development plan is learning: how the person in question can acquire new capabilities in a set of identified areas, keeping in mind the need for both competence and interpersonal/leadership skills. First, a note about the *setting* in which a person gains new skills. For potential family employees, there is high value in building capabilities *outside* the family firm before joining it, whether in a similar industry as the family business or not. This enables young professionals to build skills in a context in which their last name does not set them apart. They thus have the opportunity to experiment and make mistakes in an organization free of "family memory." They get accustomed to receiving "real" performance feedback in this environment, so it becomes a natural part of their work experience. It also helps them hit the ground running and contribute more quickly when they arrive at the family business.

Second, many family firms we have observed, especially those in the early stages, tend to avoid relying on formal learning plans, taking more of a "figure it out as we go along" approach. These firms tend to assume that people—family and nonfamily employees—will

Table 7.3   Learning domains in the business and family

Learning Domains in the Business	Level	Learning Domains in the Family
• Leadership vision and values • Strategic thinking • Execution of strategy • Operations and financial management • Change management • Effective governance	Enterprise	• Stewardship • Letting go and passing the baton • Financial and risk management • Community and philanthropic endeavors • Ownership structures (e.g., shareholders agreements, dividend policies) • Effective governance
• Our markets—past and present • Key events in our business • Key players in our history • Our teamwork and collaboration • Our ability to continuously improve	Team and Family	• Our family's history—the good, the bad and the ugly • Influential family members—past and present • Our ability to work together as a family—making decisions and collaborating • Our involvement of spouses
• My technical/professional skills • My business knowledge • My initiative, judgment, and curiosity	Individual	• My communication style and preferences • My role in the family, e.g., sibling position, generation, gender • My role as a family member working in the business

pick up the skills and knowledge they need through experience and exposure, rather than *planned, deliberate learning*. Although this approach often works to some degree during the early phases of a business, it can fall short as the company and family grow and become more complex and diverse. A lack of systematic, repeatable learning mechanisms can impede the development of innovation and fresh thinking. In addition to providing a basis for strategic change, training and other formal programs—whether internal or external—can help employees understand the firm's way of doing things, including with regard to values and culture. This can apply to family as well as nonfamily employees. For example, a second-generation business family daughter we know did an internship at her family's retail business and underwent training as part of her onboarding experience. "When my manager went over the company's values and how to live them, I recognized them immediately as the values I'd grown up with," she said. Rather than seeing the training as redundant or unnecessary, she was thankful that it reinforced her family's longstanding values and placed them in the context of working for the family firm.

Competence-focused learning. Competence-focused learning approaches focus on the specific technical or management skills needed to perform in one's job. As mentioned earlier, competence- and interpersonal skills can overlap, for example with regard to communications skills or presentation capabilities. While the exact vehicle used to gain competence-related capabilities is less important than the motivation to do so, here are several categories of sources for such learning:

- *Courses/seminars/workshops/conferences.* Courses and workshops, like books, are available on virtually any topic you can think of, including those related to family business. There are one-day seminars on applying Six Sigma approaches to manufacturing, online courses on how to be a better manager, and week-long, on-site courses in specific family business topics. Many family business centers housed within a university offer family business workshops. Northwestern University's Kellogg School of Management, for example, offers separate week-long seminars on family enterprise governance and leadership (along with workshops and conferences on other family business areas and general business topics). Sauder's School of Business at the University of British Columbia offers customizable workshops on topics from managing change and transition to leadership and relationship management. Several family firms we have observed require participation in these seminars for rising family and nonfamily leaders.[10] Family owners and employees of Joseph Phelps Vineyards take advantage of external learning opportunities, including classes on family business dynamics/processes, seminars from local law firms, and customized sessions led by family business consultants.

- *Coaching/mentorship.* Coaching, as discussed at length in the next section, is a valuable, customized source of learning. A coach can be a manager, another colleague, or an outside professional (such as an independent director) with expertise in multiple areas and, in many cases, rich experience to draw on for advice. Fit is, of course, an important dimension of coaching, and here too we return to the idea of competence and interpersonal skills. A good coach will be competent in the areas that matter—whether strategy, marketing, manufacturing, technology, or communication, among others—but also relate well to the person being coached and ideally serve as a role model for interpersonal/leadership capabilities. We learn best from those whom we respect, admire, and see as having some common ground with us. The two third-generation employees of Joseph Phelps Vineyards, for example, are mentored informally by two independent board members.
- *Rotational programs.* Rotational programs involve moving people, especially rising leaders, through a series of different jobs representing diverse functions and responsibilities firm-wide. Such programs are popular—especially for family employees—because they promote learning about many areas in a short period of time. This can help the individual develop a broad network of contacts across the firm quickly. Short rotational assignments can help an individual identify their areas of best fit, where they can contribute the most value while pursuing their interests. At the same time, too much moving around may result in developing only a superficial understanding of key issues and processes, and might prevent the taking on of real Profit & Loss responsibility and risk. This can present an unrealistic view of the work (for example, the rotating employee rarely has to endure tedious jobs). So aiming for the right kind of rotational program or experience is important. Here, the 80/20 approach described previously might promote

the wide exposure without removing the opportunity for in-depth job responsibility.

- *Developmental assignments.* Competence can also be gained through on-the-job developmental assignments or smaller-scale projects that are not part of a formal rotation program. These are often used for more junior employees, as vehicles through which to learn from their more experienced team-mates and managers. For example, a junior family marketing professional can be invited as a member of a team developing a forecast for next year's sales and marketing budget, and given specific tasks that can help build their marketing, finance, and teamwork/communication skills. Even rising leaders and more senior professionals can learn from developmental assignments outside their area of career focus. And nonfamily executives might be invited to work on family-related tasks with fellow executives and/or the board—such as ensuring continuity of the business's values and culture into the next generation—to boost their skills and awareness in these important areas.

- *Shadowing.* A less active but still important form of competence-focused learning involves shadowing, or observing specific colleagues, teams, or governance bodies in action, to under-stand the skills required to have an impact in multiple areas. This can be useful for junior and higher-level colleagues alike, depending on their development needs. Several family firms we know have "Board Observer" positions on their boards and family councils, to allow rising, next-generation family mem-bers to learn from these governance bodies for a year or more before moving into full director roles including voting rights and/or fiduciary accountability. During that period they gain skills related to governance, management, and communication through careful observation.

- *Books.* Books, like the one you are reading now, can be a focused, cost-effective way to gain skill-related knowledge and insights in any domain of business. An Amazon search for the keyword "business" returns 2,597,733 results![11] There are books on everything from manufacturing practices to marketing strategies to management policies. The challenge, of course, is finding the most relevant text for your development needs. Recommendations from colleagues and professionals you admire can provide direction, as can online searches for recommendations in a given area. Perhaps most important is ensuring that the material is actually read, digested, and *applied* to real-life situations. High-quality coaching and feedback, as discussed in the next section, can help make that happen. The siblings of one family we work with formed a book club in which they choose four to six family business books/resources to review each year and meet quarterly to discuss.

See the "Project-Based Learning at Joseph Phelps Vineyards" Box for an example of learning through developmental assignments.

Project-Based Learning at Joseph Phelps Vineyards

In late 2014, family-owned Joseph Phelps Vineyards adopted a professional development program for the two third-generation cousins working in the business. As part of the program, the young professionals are working on special projects in areas that include finance, HR, information technology (IT), and energy. "We are gaining exposure to a lot of different people and a bigger picture perspective on everything that goes on in the business," said third-generation employee Will Phelps. For example, he will be working on capital budgeting with the CFO and director of operations. Will and his cousin Elizabeth Neuman were working together on a go-to-market plan with the VP of Sales and Marketing, and that project included collaborating with a team of outside salespeople. Elizabeth is working independently with HR to help develop a management training program (for family and nonfamily employees). Both Will and Elizabeth anticipate being part of a near-term effort to revamp the business's website. The cousins spend up to 10 percent of their time on these special projects, and present their progress and recommendations related to each to the board. In this way, the third-generation members are learning quickly about multiple functions and activities while contributing value to their family business. Elizabeth pointed out that the program is not only helping them gain skills but also strengthening their relationship as collaborators. In noting that it was important to have strong development programs for both family and nonfamily employees, she said, "Everyone wants the opportunity to learn."

It is important to note that development of competence is not just for individuals. It is also important for your firm to gain *collective competence* in everything from strategy and finance to communication and HR (presumably the reason you are reading this book). As noted above, some family firms, especially those with tremendous success in early stages, develop a belief that they cannot learn much from outside parties. We want to emphasize that investment in learning, including the organizational variety, from *all* sources is paramount. For example, online resources and conferences related to talent development can be found through organizations like the Association for Talent Development.[12]

But boosting your organizational development skills also involves asking important questions such as these:

- Do we have learning systems in place?
- What unique learning systems do we need that are related to being a family business?
- How does learning differ for family members versus nonfamily members?
- How much do we invest (dollars or percentage of total spending) in development?
- How do we assess the effectiveness of our development systems?

The answers to these questions will depend on your firm's exact situation, goals, needs, values, and culture. But the important thing is to ask them in the first place, and to explore the issues they represent, with a focus on constant evolution.

Interpersonal/leadership-focused learning. This type of learning is about the "softer, squishier" skills that are much more important than many realize. Often, the soft stuff is indeed the harder stuff. For example, the ability to communicate, provide feedback, or resolve stubborn conflict is often seen as more innate and harder to learn. We believe that, while some individuals may naturally be more capable in these soft skills, such capabilities can be strengthened through thoughtful, comprehensive development.

As discussed in previous chapters, including "Selection," it is critical to *hire* for interpersonal abilities or emotional intelligence (what we labeled "chemistry" in that chapter), as aligned with your firm's specific values and culture. Good selection can promote good chemistry among the individuals and groups in your firm. But even with careful selection, people who are strongest on interpersonal/leadership skills can learn and grow, especially as their responsibilities increase. Similarly, pushing hard on your firm's cultural features, as discussed in the "Culture" chapter, can also boost what can be thought of as "collective chemistry"—or the fit and synergy between individuals and teams—as this will infuse every element of your people's experience over time with the values and norms upheld by your firm.

Beyond those general approaches, more specific ways of boosting interpersonal/leadership-focused learning include the vehicles for competence listed above, such as books, courses/seminars, coaching (including peer coaching), and forum groups focused on topics like leadership and communication skills. We also want to point out the benefits of a low-cost "buddy" system in which newer employees can be paired with experienced colleagues as informal coaches and mentors—with special attention paid to choosing coaches who exemplify strong interpersonal skills or emotional intelligence. Such a system enables new people to learn a great deal by observing these "living examples," whether how to conduct oneself in meetings and other interactions, how to navigate hierarchies within the family or business, and/or how to handle political issues within the family firm. Of course, such mentors can be valuable for teaching competence-related skills as well, beyond the transmission of culture, values, and behavior. New family employees may benefit deeply from being paired with a more experienced family member at the firm. One of the cousins at a third-generation family food company we know has been deputized to play this role because she is a naturally communicative, considerate, and high-energy person who takes pleasure in helping junior colleagues, whether family or not, find their way at the business.

Coaching and Feedback

As depicted in our earlier visual, learning and coaching/feedback form a "cycle within a cycle" such that people, guided by their development plans, learn from multiple sources and gain regular feedback and coaching as they apply what they have learned. This iterative loop within the broader development cycle ensures people are more likely to apply what they learn in the first place and to do so in the most effective way, learning from coaches, mentors, and other feedback sources as they go.

Feedback. Feedback is a challenging issue for most organizations. Employees at all levels say they want more feedback, but most organizations do not provide feedback well, benefiting neither the employee nor the firm. A recent *Harvard Business Review* article highlighted the issue starkly by showing that while "no one wants to give negative feedback, everyone wants to hear it."[13] In fact, the international respondents to the authors' survey about feedback agreed that negative feedback improves performance more than positive feedback by a three-to-one margin. It is no surprise that negative feedback is hard to come by—or any feedback at all, for that matter. As humans, we are often reluctant to share our feelings, negative or positive, about others. It can feel like an unnatural, uncomfortable process, especially when there is little precedent for it, even when positioned as coming from a place of mutual respect. This can be especially true about feedback in a work setting, and it is even more complicated for family firms, because the feedback providers and/or recipients may be family members.

Both provider and recipient can be part of the problem. Providers may be reluctant, as noted above, but recipients can also make the process tough. At one family firm, the third-generation daughter disagreed vehemently with any constructive feedback she received from anyone and routinely complained to her siblings about it. You can imagine the kind of negative environment that created at the business and among the broader family. Such patterns are best addressed through a culture that emphasizes the benefits of feedback achieved through accountability and candor.

Because feedback is such a vital element of development, it is important to build it into your system. Feedback will, of course, be part of the formal performance evaluation process discussed in the "Performance Assessment" section. Additionally, informal, ongoing feedback is vital for high performance, along with effective systems promoting regular, constructive feedback. A prerequisite for constructive feedback is a values-based culture that creates the proper context for feedback: one of respect and genuine care for employees' welfare. In that context, feedback is a powerful vehicle for support and improvement, rather than some form of false praise, punishment, or personal attack.

One-on-one feedback can and should happen formally, but it can also happen informally, and frequently. The challenge is that delivery of feedback is no easy feat (as discussed above), and most people have little training in this area. Moreover, the provision of low-quality feedback creates both short- and long-term issues, potentially as part of a vicious cycle: job-related expectations are communicated inadequately, contributing to poor performance, which results in a largely negative performance review with ineffective feedback and communication of expectations, and so it begins again. In contrast, effective provision of feedback can be part of a *virtuous* cycle that results in successively stronger individual performance and impact.

One way to make one-on-one feedback more effective is to *focus on behavior versus general, more personally directed assessments of a situation.* "There are times when your work could benefit from better organization" will be received in a more positive way—and likely acted upon—than "You are not an organized person." Here, the development cycle component of learning figures in because, while some people are naturally more adept at providing (or receiving) feedback than others, it is a skill that can be enhanced through formal or informal programs, including the simple idea of focusing on specific behaviors.

A special case of feedback provision in family firms is when a family member must report to another family member. We generally advise families to avoid this situation, but sometimes there is no viable alternative, such as when a second-generation member rises to a level of reporting to the first-generation founder or senior executive. Here, the same ideas apply:

- Feedback should be part of a culture of mutual support and respect.
- It should be delivered with sensitivity and tact.
- It should focus more on behaviors than generalized assessments.
- It should be as specific and actionable as possible.
- It should be positive and forward looking rather than negative and focused on the past (e.g., "You would add more value to

this company if you did more/less of X going forward" rather than "You have done too much [or not enough] of X in the past.").

- It should be supplemented by feedback from others including nonfamily members, as discussed below. Nonfamily business leaders and board members are particularly valuable sources of feedback for family employees, including as part of a family employment advisory committee.
- It should be candid and frank as possible, though family and nonfamily may be understandably hesitant in this regard.

Getting one-on-one feedback right in your family firm will contribute to a culture of openness and constant evolution not just for the family members in question but for the entire organization.

While one-on-one feedback from managers, coaches, and mentors is valuable, it can sometimes result in too narrow or extreme a view. As such, we emphasize the value of a *360-degree feedback process*. This involves gaining a variety of perspectives on an individual's performance and impact from a broad range of parties, depending on the role and level of the person in question:

- direct reports
- peers
- managers
- board members (especially independent/outside directors)
- customers/suppliers
- family owners

Getting at the right set of feedback involves seeking a wide range of responses, including from those who would offer constructive comments and insights. It is important to avoid those individuals who provide *only* superficial and/or positive feedback. As you may recall from our discussion above, negative feedback is viewed as being more related to performance improvement than unrealistic positive feedback. It is also important to try to secure multiple providers of feedback from different sources, for a more complete view of performance.

A 360-degree feedback process is especially important for family firms because it can result in more honest, higher-quality insights about the performance of family employees. In fact, it can be interesting to break down the feedback received about family employees based on its source: family or nonfamily feedback-providers—as long as there is a sufficient number of feedback providers to keep the sources anonymous! Potential trends might include the tendency for family employees to go too easy—or too hard—on one another, depending in part on family dynamics and firm culture.

There are multiple methods through which to implement a 360-degree feedback program. These include computerized measures, which promote anonymity, easy organization, and analysis of the feedback captured. Firms can also customize online tools to measure what they value most, or even create their own in-house 360-degree feedback assessment. We have observed that debriefing the results of 360-degree measures is often best handled by an *outside party*, to ensure objectivity and avoid bias or perceptions of bias. For example, the second-generation son of a family business owner we know was reluctant to hear feedback from managers (including his father) because he felt they would judge him unfairly (positively or negatively), given his position in the family. But he was receptive to hearing the results of a 360-degree program implemented by an outside firm, and his performance improved considerably after he incorporated the feedback into his work. Despite recent debates about the merits of 360-degree feedback systems—including as related to poor participation of key evaluators (like managers), vague forms/instructions, and personal rather than constructive responses—we are strong advocates of a *properly implemented* program of this nature in the family firm.[14]

Feedback is taken very seriously at Joseph Phelps Vineyards. "People may think family members don't get constructive criticism, but we definitely do," said third-generation family employee Will Phelps. Performance feedback is delivered as part of a structured annual review and check-in meeting led by the national sales manager (Will's manager) and the sales/marketing VP. "We really want feedback about finite goals like sales targets," said his cousin and colleague Elizabeth Neuman, "but also about other things like leadership and self-improvement." This notion is very much in line with our emphasis on promoting learning in the competence and interpersonal/leadership domains.

Coaching. Because much of the earlier content in this chapter touches on elements of coaching, we will summarize the topic briefly here. Formal and informal coaching are essential components of a strong development system, and a critical part of an individual and a collective learning process. In fact, coaching itself is a form of learning, as coaches and mentors generate insights and suggestions for best practices in the domains of competence and interpersonal/leadership capabilities, based on their prior experience.

While the best coaches are those with an interest in helping others, a strong base of experience, and basic skills related to sensitivity and communication, we are especially in favor of using family employees or long-standing nonfamily employees/directors as coaches and mentors where feasible, as they can communicate ideas on competence and interpersonal skills through the lens of the family's values and culture. For example, at a Canadian retail firm, the CEO is retiring soon, but has pledged to serve as an ongoing mentor for the next-generation family business leaders, especially with regard to values. Rather than taking a rigid approach to values transmission, the outgoing leader recognizes that each generation and individual will translate the family's values into ideas and actions that make sense for their specific business situation, goals, and work style. So in this sense, strong mentors help mentees successfully resolve the typical family business paradox of honoring the past while living in the present, among other issues.

The mentorship of outside directors has been particularly valuable for the third-generation employees of Joseph Phelps Vineyards. "My mentor has good perspective on family business in general and acts as an unbiased third party who gives good advice and really grounds me," said Will Phelps.

Some family firms have had success promoting the learning and development of employees by having an *internal sponsor*, senior to the employee, who is specifically responsible for looking within the business for developmental opportunities. So along with serving as a mentor, the sponsor is a champion or advocate for the employee in looking for opportunities for them to demonstrate and stretch their capabilities. The role could be called out as part of a manager's responsibilities or it could be someone else within the employee's team.

In general, coaches in a family business not only help their individual charges grow but also broker stronger relationships between the incumbent and incoming generations, such that these groups can work together toward a unified vision and mission, driven by shared values. In this regard, we see the strongest coaches as representing and stimulating in others the quality of *humble audacity,* a combination of humility and bravery that can help the organization chart a new course without forgetting its roots. The most effective family firms we know actively seek and cultivate humble audacity in their people, and create space for the related coaching and day-to-day interactions that yield growth across dimensions.

In short, the exact parameters of coaching in the family business are less important than providing ample opportunities for the development of formal and informal coaching relationships at every level.

Pitfalls

The largest pitfall related to development is inertia, or the failure to expend the effort needed to create a comprehensive, effective development system. Family businesses fall into the trap of working hard "in" the business, thus leaving little time to work "on" the business. Sometimes families ignore the need for a development system, in part because they do not recognize its value or believe they do not have the capabilities to create the right one. As we have emphasized throughout this book, it is better to start with something than not to start at all. In creating and refining your development system, beware these common pitfalls and stumbling blocks.

- *Mistaking "different" for bad.* This is especially relevant to new leaders. Sometimes they are seen as needing development because their style or perspective departs from that of the incumbent leader, especially when the former leader is the business founder. A good development system will help you separate different from ineffective or suboptimal, recognizing the kind of change that can be good or even necessary for the firm and creating rewards for the results such leadership can generate.

- *Falling off the balance beam.* Developing talent is a challenging balancing act, especially when it comes to family employees. We find that many firms err on one extreme or the other, such as being overly supportive ("We just want to help you succeed and will be infinitely patient.") or tough ("Succeed fast, or else."). The best approach strikes the right balance, setting high standards, but in the context of meaningful support and encouragement. It can also mean creating learning opportunities that are outside of the person's comfort zone but not unmanageable. Aiming for good balance is part of an effective development system.

- *Creating a development system in a vacuum.* Some firms have development systems or standards, but fail to connect these to their mission, strategy, or culture. "We need to have a training program," the leaders might say, and go about creating a program without taking into account what is best for the firm. Not surprisingly, such programs tend to be ineffective and are often abandoned. Rather than thinking about development in a vacuum, start with the broader vision and goals of your firm and seek to align the system with these. This vacuum could also apply to next-generation family members who only develop within their own family business system rather than gaining valuable outside experience. This experience not only brings fresh ideas back into their own family business but also serves to build the family member's capabilities in different ways.

Things to Remember

Development is a critical, often overlooked component of the HR lifecycle in family business. Here are the main things to remember from this chapter.

- Development is especially important in family firms because a good development system ensures the highest return on human capital, along with fostering a healthy relationship among family and nonfamily employees, creating a strong bench of talent and reinforcing a culture of learning and constant evolution.

- We see development as a continuous cycle of assessment, learning, and coaching, a dynamic process with the following components:
  - *Performance Evaluation and Gap Analysis:* Evaluation should be based on job description/expectations, with a range of possible approaches extending from informal to highly formal reviews. We recommend an objective, standardized approach that considers traditional outcomes and interpersonal/process-related variables. Ideally, the evaluation would highlight competence and interpersonal/leadership skills, as well as, a means of addressing any gapsas part of a customized development plan.
  - *Outcomes:* Positive and negative outcomes result from the performance evaluation, including rewards, demotions, and termination. It is important to understand that the form and delivery of such outcomes reflects your firm's culture, and that this is a particularly critical area in which to separate business and family—the same outcome-related criteria should apply to family and nonfamily employees.
  - *Development planning:* Such planning is aimed at finding learning opportunities that will address skill gaps and build on strengths. Successors, future owners, and nonfamily executives warrant a highly strategic approach to their development. We recommend that future owner employees spend about 20 percent of their time developing ownership skill (such as observing board meetings and participating in family business conferences/exchanges).
  - *Learning:* Learning can and should take place at the individual, team, and organizational levels, for both the family and the business. We endorse having family members gain meaningful experience outside the business before joining, and to make use of planned, deliberate learning programs within the business for both competence-focused learning and interpersonal/leadership skill development. Courses, coaches, and rotational programs are all effective methods.
  - *Coaching and feedback:* In our model, coaching/feedback forms a "cycle within a cycle" within the learningprocess, one that can boost and accelerate development. Feedback, especially the negative variety, is often avoided, but can be

delivered strategically as part of one-on-one interactions (including between family employees, when necessary) and 360-degree assessments that provide a more holistic view. Experienced family employees and longstanding nonfamily managers and directors all make effective coaches. These individuals help mentees develop, while fostering strong relationships between generations and among family and nonfamily employees.

- Development-related pitfalls include assuming development will happen on its own and failing to connect development systems adequately to your firm's mission, strategy, or culture.

8

Exit

Penny Andrews, CEO of Smart Start Pet Products, could not believe what she was seeing. A friend had called early that morning to alert her to an online story about the company. Within minutes Penny found the story—"Smart Start Poisons Pets"—posted on an anonymous website: www.stayawayfromsmartstart.com. The site alleged that Smart Start routinely used dangerous chemicals in its pet food products, and that consumers should avoid purchasing and using the products. Over 50 people had commented on the site, mostly to say they would no longer consider using Smart Start. Minutes later, when the CEO signed into her work e-mail account, she found queries from several area reporters, asking her to comment on the allegations.

At first Penny was mystified by the damaging story, which was completely false. Who would want to hurt Smart Start? The business had been started by Penny's grandfather nearly 50 years earlier, growing from a regional player in Florida to a nationwide boutique pet product business that had about $30 million in annual sales and employed over 200 people. Then it hit her: the site, which had clearly been put together quickly, was likely the work of two employees who had left the marketing department about three weeks earlier. One was a longtime marketing manager who was competent but consistently rubbed people the wrong way, whether colleagues, partners (such as Start Smart's ad agency), or customers, openly criticizing others' work or disparaging them behind their backs. The other was a more junior employee and more recent hire who had handled the business's social media. The younger man reported to the marketing manager in question, and the two had become friends.

Recently, the manager's negative behavior had crossed a new line. Frustrated with his perception of inaction on the part of his VP boss, the manager had gone ahead on his own and executed a contract for 12 months of advertising with an online advertising broker. None of the required approval signatures for the expenditure had been gathered, and the strategy was clearly counter to that set by the VP Marketing. Penny and the VP had decided to ask the manager to resign, citing the established pattern of negative behavior and action taken beyond his stated authority. He resisted at first, but eventually agreed, because he "didn't want to work somewhere like this anyway." Later that week, the junior colleague quit, telling colleagues he disagreed with the way the company had handled his manager's departure.

As Penny looked into options to address the slanderous content—now confident she had discerned its source—she also began to analyze why it had happened in the first place. She realized that she had waited too long to deal with the problem. In fact, Penny recognized that the way the company handled issues related to exit was far from optimal, with no real system in place. That had become an issue not only recently but also some years earlier when her cousin, an operations manager, had decided to leave the family business for a higher-level position at a consumer food company. It had been unclear how to communicate that decision to the firm, and whether to discuss the possibility of re-entry at a later date. Now the cousin was interested in rejoining the family business, and Penny was not sure how to handle that. While the firm had a small HR department, it was not very helpful in this regard. The group had always been focused on more transactional issues, such as paperwork related to hiring, payroll, and benefits. Moreover, there had always been confusion and tension about how best to handle performance and exit-related issues for family employees versus their nonfamily peers. The more she thought about it, the more the CEO recognized she needed a much more thoughtful exit management system to address all of these issues.

*   *   *

Exit management, the final phase of the HR lifecycle, is a critical component of family business, but one that most people would rather not deal with. The reality is that there are large consequences for failing to create best practices related to employee departures. Consider that more than two million US employees quit their jobs in any given month. That figure, which does not even include involuntary terminations, is growing.[1] In Canada, 51 percent of those polled indicated that they had not held their current job for more than two years.[2] In Organization for Economic Cooperation and Development 1 (OECD1) countries (those with the highest level of economic development), up to 15 percent of employees quit their jobs every year.[3] Given the number of departures, and as the example above suggests, handling exits carefully is important for any business. Employee departures have practical, legal, and cultural implications for your firm. Even something as simple as an exit interview can improve the departure experience for all parties and provide valuable information about how to enhance the ongoing experience of people who remain with your business.[4]

Managing exits carefully is paramount for family firms for several reasons:

- *It promotes—or damages—trust and relationship building.* If you are able to deal with conflict well, including that related to departures, it helps you build greater trust and stronger relationships within the family and the business. In contrast, a failure to manage departures well, especially those of family employees, can implode the family and result in longer term damage. We know of many examples in which families struggled for years to recover from the departure of even one family employee under suboptimal circumstances.

- *It's a "3-Circle" issue.* In the beginning of the book, we referred to the 3-Circle framework, which consists of three interacting systems in a family business: (1) family (including all family members, whether they own shares or not); (2) ownership (anyone holding equity in the firm); and (3) business (including all those employed in the business).[5] Because people can be part of more than one circle (and some are members of all three circles), it is important to ensure that their departure from one circle (for our purposes, the business system) does not become an exit from the overall family enterprise system. For example, when a deeply dissatisfied family member opts to leave the family firm, she may also stop attending family events such as birthdays, holidays, and the like, and even consider selling her shares in the business. Sadly, this is not a hypothetical example.

- *It affects everyone—and the business's reputation.* The impact of sound "exit management" goes well beyond the specific managers and employees directly involved. *Any* employee may observe or hear about how exits are handled, and this influences their perception and experience of the firm's culture and practices. Outsiders may also learn about exit-related practices, especially with the rising trend of sharing work-related experiences through social media. This can affect the firm's reputation, which can have a ripple effect on everything from revenues to recruiting to retention. Because many family firms take pride in and reap benefits from treating employees as family, they may take even greater interest in managing exits well. Moreover, because many family businesses are longstanding, visible pillars of their community, they need to be highly sensitive to any issues that impact their reputation.
- *The link between exit management and performance.* The ability to manage exits well demonstrates the firm's ability—and willingness—to address performance issues proactively and effectively, setting higher expectations for performance. Avoiding the challenges related to exits sends an implicit message that lower performance will be tolerated or overlooked.
- In short, poorly managed exits can cause issues on multiple fronts for your business and family, and taking a proactive approach to this matter is critical.[6]

Exit as a Transition, Not an Event

Exits are hard. It is human nature to cling to the familiar, to be uncomfortable with the unknown, whether with regard to work, relationships, or other areas. Think of making an exit as jumping from one trapeze to another. There are three stages to this transition: letting go of the old job/position (or the bar, in the case of the trapeze), landing somewhere new (such as a new job, or a literal or figurative safety

Figure 8.1 The three stages of exit.

net), and being suspended in the "in-between," which can seem like an eternity, depending on how far away the next destination (trapeze bar) is (Figure 8.1).[7] Most of us have trouble with one, two, or all three of these transition points (which may explain why most of us have never attempted to swing from a trapeze, or certainly not to jump from one to another!). We also want to emphasize that in many cases it is difficult not only for an employee to move toward exit—though two million people change jobs monthly in the United States, we would guess that many more consider exiting their jobs, but choose not to—but also for businesses to take steps to make exits happen. Letting go and moving on is hard for everyone.

Because exits pose such challenges, the tendency on the part of both individuals and businesses is to avoid and/or delay exits or occasionally to rush them. Inertia is one of the strongest forces with which we have to contend, and many of us put off changes, including positive ones, much longer than we should.[8] However, it can be tempting to force exits to happen more quickly than they should, or to fail to develop a mind-set and system for handling departures because this takes time and effort in the short term. It may also be tempting to think that your business systems, such as a strong performance management system including regular formal reviews, will help prevent the need for exits, or at least make them rare and generally mutual. In reality, most exits are likely to be complex, challenging, and even messy. There is no easy way around that fact, and accepting it is a key step to improving how you handle exits.

In this context, we encourage you to see exits not as an event but as a *transition*. While the actual departure of an employee can be considered a time-limited event, exits represent an ongoing complex process involving multiple types of reorientation for all parties.[9] Just as succession, or the rise of a new leader or leaders within the business, is more of a process than an event, so too is a departure. It is not just that a person vacates their seat or leaves their team/role but also that the business loses their presence, their impact, and their influence, with both practical and more symbolic implications. And, as both the departing employee and the business are transitioning from one state to another, it is important to apply our ongoing theme of *constant evolution* to this area, as well. The nominal change associated with an exit (an empty chair) may be quick, but the transition it represents can and should be a more deliberate, careful process. This is especially true for family firms, which tend to place a higher value on people and take a longer term orientation than do nonfamily firms. Taking a more deliberative approach to exit is also aligned with our overall view of HR as a series of ongoing processes that aggregate into the culture and experience of working in the family firm, rather than representing a group of disconnected, discrete events.

A strategic, effective departure process can and will create lasting value for all parties, including those not directly involved in the exit (such as the employees who stay with the business). So rather than putting off dealing with any kind of exit, we strongly advocate taking steps to make the process of departure as conscious, explicit, and mindful as possible. That means supporting and even welcoming the exit process as something from which everyone can benefit and learn.

This chapter will help you take a more proactive, systematic approach to exit, using helpful frameworks and practical ideas.

Two Kinds of Exits

As a first step to managing exits strategically, it is important to understand the two main categories they fall into: voluntary and not-so-voluntary.

Voluntary exits are just that—when an employee opts to leave the company, rather than being asked or forced to. That is an easy concept to understand at a basic level, but the reasons underlying a voluntary departure can be complex and multidimensional, with many ramifications for family firms. This kind of exit can result from both positive and negative motivations, as suggested by the lists below.

Positive Reasons for Voluntary Exit

- to seek further education (such as an MBA)
- to accept a (higher) position outside the family business (potentially with the intent of returning to the family firm at some point in the future)
- to pursue a new direction, personal passion, adventure, or other desired life change
- to spend more time with family or care for a family member
- to move to a new geography that is a better fit for the person's life needs
- to retire

Negative Reasons for Voluntary Exit

- dissatisfaction with position/responsibilities/advancement (related to next point)
- lured away by a competitor that offers a better situation with regard to salary, responsibilities, culture, coworkers, location, job challenge, growth opportunity, or other factors
- challenging family dynamics within the business
- poor health, burnout, exhaustion
- poor job and/or culture fit
- limited growth opportunities
- perception of poor leadership (lack of recognition, autonomy, ability to contribute in a meaningful way)

Obviously, a combination of positive and negative factors can motivate a given individual's decision to exit, whether a family or nonfamily employee. Regardless of the specific motivation, here are several suggestions related to voluntary exits:

- *Do not take the exit personally.* The second-generation CEO of a large transportation business in the southern United States always took employee exits very personally, especially when it was a family member, even if it was for the best for the business and individual in question. "It just feels like a betrayal," she told fellow owners. While we understand that this can be a natural reaction to a departure, with family member exits, a departure from the employee "circle" should not necessitate an exit from the other two circles: family and ownership (although there are some shareholder agreements that only allow ownership by family members working in the business). Such exits, especially when unexpected and/or by a higher level family employee, will certainly require adjustment, but can be handled mindfully and effectively, with coaching from HR as needed, using some of the ideas presented below. A careful approach may not reduce the pain of an exit, but may help make it feel less personal and create a learning opportunity for the family and the business. Overall, it is important to understand that a departure is based on a specific set of circumstances at a specific point in time, rather than representing a general rejection of the business. Moreover, if someone believes they would be more satisfied elsewhere, their departure is probably a *good* thing for the firm, though it may involve some adjustment.

- *Consider limiting the number of times an employee can enter and exit the company.* Baseball and many criminal courts have a three-strikes rule. Should your business have a similar policy when it comes to voluntary exits? We think this is a valid question to ask and seriously consider. As with many complex queries, the right answer is "it depends." Whether or not you should limit the number of voluntary exits depends largely on the reason people may tend to come and go, especially family members, which to some degree is based on the culture of your business. Do family employees use employment with the business as a "safety net" (in line with the trapeze analogy suggested earlier)? If so, do they use this fallback option sparingly or abuse it? Alternatively, do employees grow, professionally or personally, from time away and add greater value to the company upon re-entry? The answers to those questions can help you determine whether to institute a limit on voluntary exits (yes, if people are abusing the fallback option), what that limit might be, and how the culture of your firm might be influencing related patterns.
- *Learn from voluntary exits.* As we have emphasized throughout this book, each challenge you face and/or take on is a true

learning opportunity. A voluntary departure is no different. Ask yourself what you and your firm can learn from the exit, including how to improve the employee experience and, in turn, satisfaction and retention. Especially when losing a truly valued contributor, think about what the experience can teach you about the changes you need to make to prevent such departures in the future.

Involuntary exits are those decided by someone other than the departing employee. Consider the example of an eastern Canadian midsized family business in consumer goods: the middle son was a successful salesman for the company, but he showed an increasingly poor work ethic (arriving late for appointments and meetings) and instances of poor judgment (such as inappropriate humor), and was eventually asked to leave the firm by the CEO (his uncle) after multiple instances and several complaints. This is largely an example of poor chemistry (recall that we break down sources of employee value into competence and chemistry), which is one of the motivators of involuntary exit on the list below:

- low competence to fulfill job responsibilities
- poor chemistry (communication and interpersonal skills, poor cultural fit)
- unaddressed mental health or addiction issues
- downsizing (layoffs required by the business situation, rather than employee-specific factors)
- restructuring (i.e., acquisitions, new strategic direction, growth, and the like)
- low motivation, leading to poor job performance

Below we present several tips related to involuntary exits:

- *Avoid "overstayed welcomes."* Family firms, in our experience and that of many of our colleagues, tend to tolerate under-performance—whether related to competence, chemistry, or both—for too long. This is true for both family and nonfamily employees, in part because family businesses often treat everyone like family, and it can be a lot harder to fire a family member than an employee. Many of the businesses with which we have worked recognize this issue, but still struggle to address it. One of the best solutions is a strong development system that includes regular formal and informal performance conversations, as discussed previously in the "Development" chapter. In general, you need to be able to "discuss the undiscussables," and take action, as suggested by the next point.

- *Discuss the undiscussables.* Part of the problem behind overstayed welcomes is an unwillingness (or inability) to discuss issues such as underperformance and unmet expectations. Again, this is often linked to the family part of family business, as families often leave important things unspoken in order to avoid short-term pain and anxiety. As suggested above, a strong development system is one way to address this problem by making the process of providing performance feedback a regular and expected experience. More broadly, a culture that supports open communication and honesty will provide the foundation for discussion and resolution of sensitive topics. HR can be a key partner in helping the family broach difficult topics, whether by facilitating discussion or bringing in outside resources to help with this. Family meetings can also be an important venue in which the family can reinforce the importance and need for high performance from family members working in the family business.

- *Know when to fire someone.* Part of the problem with involuntary exits is that it is hard to know when exactly it is worth ending a relationship with an employee. There can be so much subjectivity related to job performance—not to mention legal concerns—that it often becomes easier to avoid the issue altogether, fail to discuss the undiscussables, and end up with highly overstayed welcomes, as discussed above. Having some sort of tool or framework in place to understand when it is time to let go can be very helpful. The "Employee Cost-Benefit Assessment Worksheet" highlights one tool that has been proposed, but many others are possible, and it is important to customize one to your company's needs and culture.

The worksheet (Table 8.1) is a simplified version of one presented by Alison Rimm and Celia Brown in a *Harvard Business Review* article.[10] It can be used as a starting point for thinking about what would work best for your firm.

Table 8.1   An employee cost-benefit assessment worksheet

Score the employee on each of the following indicators using a rating scale from 1 (Low) to 5 (High).

Indicator	Score
Positive Indicators	
• Overall quality of performance	
• Value of institutional knowledge	
• Contributions to team effectiveness	
• Likelihood of improvement	
Cost of replacement	
• Disruption that would be caused by departure	
• Recruiting costs	
(A)Total Positive Indicators and Cost of Replacement	
Negative indicators	
• Risk to project/assignment delivery	
• Drain on supervisor's time/energy	
• Risk to team processes	
• Risk to department image/reputation	
• Loss of customer satisfaction	
(B) Total Negative Indicators	
Subtract A – B = Potential Exit Score	

Add the Positive Indicators and Cost of Replacement scores, and then subtract the Negative Indicators scores; a negative total score suggests it may be time to let go.

Manage Exits Strategically

Regardless of the type of exit in question—voluntary or involuntary—the most effective approach involves a thoughtful, strategic system, one built on the recognition that exit is a transition for all parties, rather than an event. In this section we consider the components of an effective exit-management system based on three temporal phases: before, during, and after the exit.

Before the Exit

As we have hopefully made clear by now, exit from a family business can be a chaotic, ambiguous, anxiety-provoking process. This is especially the case when an exit is unexpected and/or under less-than-ideal circumstances. Careful planning *before* exits happen can go a long way toward mitigating the negative effects. Below are several practices to build your capacity to manage exits well, as the goal is strategic management rather than total elimination of departures.

Develop a transition plan. Exit is a two-way issue, with both the employee and the business moving on to new states. So it is important to know how the business will fill in for lost capabilities and other resources after an employee's departure, whether a salesperson or the CEO. Who will take over their responsibilities? How will the individual's knowledge be retained or recreated? What will happen to the informal network of which they were part? Answering these and related questions before the actual exit occurs is important for continuity of performance, culture, and other dimensions within your firm. Of course, developing a transition plan is easier when the exit is planned well in advance, such as the expected retirement of a longtime CEO. But it is also critical to have elements of a plan in place for unexpected departures, especially those at higher levels, given the potential impact on the firm. Just as the US government has established a line of presidential succession for unexpected crises, so too can your business have succession plans specifying who will take over high- and lower level responsibilities should the incumbents no longer be in those positions. We encourage the development of a specific plan for exit at all levels, including transfer of responsibilities, short-term workarounds, and other components, as customized to your firm's needs, operations, and culture. (Also, documentation of processes and procedures, in writing, can be essential in preserving knowledge and performance in face of an exit.)

Get more people involved. As noted earlier, we advocate moving exit from an "undiscussable" topic (as it tends to be in many family firms) to a highly discussable one. This will ideally include conversations among multiple parties within the business. For example, the founder of a Canadian auto parts manufacturing firm was considering retirement in the intermediate future, but worried that none of his children had the capability or interest to succeed him. Rather than waiting to see if his hunch was correct—or if a successor would magically materialize—the CEO proactively started a conversation with the second generation and his leadership group about what would happen after he exited. The result was a comprehensive plan to develop potential successors, including one of his children (who was more interested in leading the business than his father had realized), along with a fallback possibility of selling the business if that was deemed optimal.

Communicate, communicate, communicate. As the example above suggests, the best exit-related planning involves strategic communication. This includes communication with the departing member, the family (if relevant), and the broader organization about the exit(s). As we have advocated throughout this book, maintaining transparency and taking the "high road" in communications is key in all contexts. It is not just the right thing to do but also makes for smart business. For example, it is important to be aware of and pay attention to informal communication about an exit (such as rumors about downsizing), as it can lead to dissatisfaction and even negative, damaging, widespread social media content. Nature abhors a vacuum, so rumors tend to fly when no announcements are made. As such, going through more formal channels, as led or supported by HR, is the best practice, as it allows you to control content and tone. For example, a company-wide announcement (through the newsletter, for example) of the departure of a valued employee with a gracious tone—"We wish Grace the best as she moves on to other opportunities"—can go a long way toward preventing rumors, while setting the right tone for exits.

How you communicate about exits should also reflect your business's core values and culture. If you pride your firm's value/culture of respect, then exit-related communications will aim to preserve the dignity of all involved (which should probably be any organization's goal). At the same time, protection of key business resources is also important. In some firms with highly valued technology systems and/or intellectual property, it is necessary for HR to escort exiting employees from the building, to preserve security. But that does not mean sacrificing the value of respect: how you communicate about and carry out exit processes can adhere to this or any other core value. Similarly, departing family members should receive the same general treatment as other exiting employees, but with some consideration for their family status, as opposed to blind application of policies. Remember: you want to keep an exit from one circle just that – an exit from one circle only (business), rather than from two or three (i.e., family or ownership). That goal is also served by avoiding disparagement of family employees—or any employee, for that matter—after they depart.

Mind the legal stuff. Family businesses, like any organization, can find themselves in trouble by not considering the legal aspects of exit before it is too late. For example, the oldest daughter of one second-generation technology business we know left the firm after several years and immediately started a competitor company that stole significant share of business from the region. That family business had not considered asking family employees to sign a noncompete agreement, partly because they underestimated the competition scenario and partly because it was uncomfortable to ask a family member to sign a legal document in this regard. This is directly related to the "discuss the undiscussables" point made earlier. Make sure necessary legal protections are in place, including documentation, contracts, and agreements related to exits before a problem arises. Follow through on the legal side with both family and nonfamily employees. Beyond noncompetes and nondisclosure agreements, many businesses have begun including agreements related to defamation, especially because of the potential damage disgruntled employees or ex-employees can cause through social media.

Support senior exits. When Pappy Van Winkle, founder of the eponymous small-batch bourbon maker, left his leadership role at age 90, he stayed connected to the company by coming in regularly to open mail.[11] A former family co-CEO of US auto parts manufacturer Fel-Pro started a tree planting business upon his retirement. Many other senior family executives move into board chair roles for the businesses they once led, or help manage philanthropic initiatives. The main idea, in keeping with this chapter's theme, is to see the exit of a senior leader as a transition: they are not just leaving a role but moving into a new one (from one trapeze to the next), which may or may not involve ongoing contact with the business. The family and HR can facilitate this transition by helping senior leaders think about an exit before it happens and plan what is next for them and the business. Such departures will likely evoke challenging issues of status and identity, given the long tenures of many family leaders and the fact that their name is literally on the door/product. As discussed in the "Neuroscience of Exits" Box, there is growing evidence for the role neuroscience plays in transitions.

The Neuroscience of Exits

Social neuroscience researchers have suggested that the human brain operates on five primary principles: status, certainty, autonomy, relatedness, and fairness.[12] It is not hard to see how each of these can be threatened during a transition such as an exit, resulting in short-term or even chronic physiological and psychological symptoms. Founders and other executives, especially, will face loss of *status* as they leave longtime leadership roles. Everyone will face *uncertainty* as part of an exit, even if they know where they are going next. *Autonomy* can be threatened as exits often involve decisions made by others. *Relatedness* shifts when anyone leaves a group, as it causes a new relationship dynamic to emerge. And questions of *fairness* are often provoked by exits, especially involuntary ones. The ideal strategy is to aim to shift the sense of threat caused by an exit from an unconscious to a conscious level, and to take steps to deal openly and proactively with associated issues and emotions, using many of the suggestions in this chapter.

Best practices related to senior manager and leader exits include the following:

- *Putting a time frame in place*: Determine when the leader will leave, well before the exit is imminent—something like five to seven years is a good planning period. Unfortunately, fewer than 5 percent of family businesses plan leadership succession well.[13]
- *Creating a written succession/transition plan*: Determine who will succeed the leader and what kind of role the leader will move into within and/or outside the firm.
- *Addressing logistical issues*: Will the departing leader keep an office in the business? Will they have access to an assistant? Will they attend any meetings, even as a guest?
- *Managing financial/compensation issues*: Determine compensation and perks in advance of an exit.
- *Matching interests to activities*: Interests and fit will play a key role in what comes next for seniors. For example, an exiting leader with a law background could stay connected to legal

issues (such as mergers and acquisitions and contract review, patents) for the firm.

The bottom line is to think ahead about senior exits, and to plan strategically and respectfully.

During the Exit

Several practices can help you manage the actual process of the exit for the benefit of all involved.

Exit interviews. An exit interview can be a comprehensive HR-led process or a less formal conversation with management. It can provide important feedback about why an employee has chosen to leave the firm and help the business improve the employee experience on multiple dimensions. We advocate voluntary exit interviews for these reasons, and also because such interviews can contribute to a positive departure process for the employee and the company. The exit "interview" can be a face-to-face conversation, written/online survey, or some combination, and will ideally be framed with some discussion of its purpose and goals (to help the employee express their views and to help the business learn from these, along with retaining some of the employee's knowledge). As part of the interview, family businesses can ask questions related to the family dimension of the business, such as "What was good/bad (or positive/difficult) about the family ownership aspect of the business?" and "How can the family make this a better place to work?" A strong exit interview process will provide value to all parties.

Outplacement. Depending on the nature of the departure, employees might receive outplacement services, or help with understanding their qualifications and finding their next position. Factors influencing the amount of outplacement provided would include the nature of the exit (voluntary or involuntary, and why), the financial resources of the firm, and the broader business circumstances (downsizing versus business as usual, for example). Outplacement is especially appropriate in a downsizing/layoff situation. Offering outplacement services to departing family employees can help to preserve the integrity/continuity of ongoing family relationships (keeping the exit confined to one circle). But in general we suggest providing outplacement support where possible, even for more "difficult" employees, as it can preserve positive relations and even prevent damaging incidents such as negative social media messages. It can also be a powerful cultural influence for those who remain in the business, as it sends the message the firm offers care and support even for those who leave.

Severance. Severance, like outplacement, may be offered to exiting employees, depending on the circumstances of departure. Sometimes it is worth paying more severance to expedite ending a difficult relationship, as the long-term benefits may outweigh the short-term costs especially when related to family members. Conducting this kind of cost-benefit analysis can help you determine the best approach to severance for a given employee. Here, we generally support treating family and nonfamily employees the same way unless special circumstances dictate otherwise.

Celebration. So far in this chapter we have framed exits largely as losses—the loss of an employee, along with their capabilities and relationships. But it is important to remember that an exit is often a cause for celebration of the employee's tangible and intangible contributions to your business. This is especially the case when the departing individual is a longtime employee, and the departure is under positive circumstances, such as retirement or the acceptance of a new position outside the firm. Beyond the typical send-off parties and gifts of gold watches, we advocate saying farewell in a deeper, more *meaningful* way. Compiling a hard copy or virtual book of photographs, memories, and stories related to the employee's experience and impact can be a low-cost, high-value way of celebrating an exit.[14] A gift customized to the departing employee's interests is another possibility. For example, the Family Business Consulting Group (where we work as consultants) hired a local opera singer to sing at the farewell party of one of the longtime consultants. It was a meaningful, memorable event for all.

After the Exit

The process you develop to manage exits does not end with the departure itself. The best exit systems include consideration of interactions with the employee in question after they have left the firm in an official capacity. Again we offer strategies for handling this stage of exit.

- *Where are they now?* A good exit system, especially at larger firms, will include some record of where the employee has gone. Knowing postdeparture placement, even if at the aggregate level, can help you in many ways, from understanding why you might be losing employees to a particular competitor, to maintaining a strong network of alumni who may become decision-makers at customer/supplier firms or even candidates for future leadership positions at your own. Of course, it may not be possible to keep track of every departing employee, but we suggest aiming to keep informal track of valued high-performers and retirees, with the goal of maintaining goodwill.

- *Not "goodbye" but "see you soon."* Just as it is important to know where former employees are now, it can also be of value to maintain some communication with them, for the purpose of networking, relationship building, and reputation. This will, of course, depend on your goals and resources. Some large family (and nonfamily) firms have regular receptions/reunions for alumni to share knowledge, hear speakers, and identify mutually beneficial opportunities related to business development, employment, and other areas. For smaller family firms or those with fewer resources, e-communications such as newsletters or online groups can be a convenient, low-cost means of keeping in touch.

- *Sometimes they return.* As suggested above, "goodbye" does not always mean forever. Re-entry of employees is common at family firms, in part because family employees are more likely to return than others. So managing re-entry carefully is important. The nature and form of a return will depend to a large extent on why the individual exited in the first place. The return of a young family employee who left to earn an MBA will be much less complex and controversial than that of an executive who left under challenging circumstances. We also know of several cases in which nonfamily employees left on a voluntary basis, grew through other positions in the industry, and returned to add significant value to their original firm. As discussed earlier, it may be wise to limit the number of re-entries, to prohibit family members from using employment with the firm as a safety net. Similarly, it would rarely make sense to offer re-entry as an option for someone who was an abusive employee, or who has been involved in criminal activity. The "Family Employee Reentry Policy" Box offers one example of a formal policy related to returning employees that incorporates these elements. One family firm we know requires family members seeking to re-enter the business to come to a family meeting and discuss candidly why they wish to return and what additional value they can bring. If there were behavioral issues with their previous employment, they need to show how they have overcome these concerns. Placement of the returning individual is another general consideration: do they re-enter at the same level as they left, for example? Our rule of thumb is to do what is best for the business first, and then what is best for the individual as an additional but secondary consideration.

Family Employee Re-entry Policy: An Example

"A family employee who leaves the company *voluntarily* but under difficult circumstances may return, but only if an appropriate position is vacant. We will not create a position for a returning family member unless management and the family council agree this is appropriate. A family member *terminated* for criminal behavior (such as theft, property damage) may not re-enter the firm. Any family member seeking to return after dismissal (for noncriminal reasons) must hold a position outside of our business for at least two years, with a verifiable record of excellent performance. The returning member must also write a one-page letter discussing why they wish to return to our firm, and how they plan to contribute to its performance and the well-being of its people. Any returning member must go through our standard hiring processes, including drug testing if deemed appropriate."

What Smart Start Did

Penny Andrews, CEO of Smart Start Pet Products, took multiple steps to improve her firm's exit management system, motivated by the damaging online story she believed a terminated marketing manager had posted. She researched options online, attended (with her HR manager) a workshop on HR best practices sponsored by a regional family business consultancy, and spoke to family firms she admired for their people-focused initiatives. The result was a departure management system with components including the following:

- *Understanding exit as a transition rather than an event:* Executives and the HR group reframed exit to be a process that could be managed, rather than a single point of departure. That helped the team begin to put practices in place to anticipate and manage exits much more strategically, learning from past experience.
- *Discussion of "undiscussables":* The company developed a policy on reviewing performance issues more candidly as part of its development system—if the same issues, whether related to competence or chemistry, arose on two consecutive reviews, the employee would be placed on a performance improvement plan targeting that area. If there was no improvement, the issue would have to be discussed with the management team—including the CEO, if it involved higher level managerial performance—including the possibility of terminating the person in question. To inform this discussion, the manager of the person filled out an "Employee Cost-Benefit Assessment Worksheet." These practices were followed for both family and nonfamily employees.
- *Communication:* Smart Start developed a much better system of communication related to exits. This included informing new employees of expectations more comprehensively when they first joined the company, including the performance-related expectations in the point above. It also meant being more transparent about any downsizing possibilities (though this had not yet happened at the company). Greater care was also taken in communication with departing employees—such as through exit interviews, where feasible—to understand their reasons for leaving, assure them the firm had their best interests in mind, and learn how to improve the employee experience for those still at the business. The business also communicated departures, especially those of higher level people, more formally, through the company's online newsletter.

- *Legal matters*: The business became much more careful with legal matters related to exit. With their attorney's help, the team developed a noncompete agreement, along with an agreement not to use social media or other online content against the company during or after employment. These agreements were explained carefully to all new employees during their onboarding process, and also covered for new employees by the HR team and area heads.

- *Re-entry policy*: Penny and her team developed a re-entry policy for employees stipulating that any employee would be considered for re-entry up to two times, assuming they left the firm in good standing. Returning family employees such as Penny's cousin would be expected to discuss their potential contributions (and any risks of their re-entry) with the family first and potentially the management team, and agree to undergo the company's standard hiring process.

The new exit management system added immediate value to Smart Start, as it made policies and practices related to departures much clearer and easier to follow for everyone in the firm. The HR group took the lead in implementing the system, with strong support from management, including Penny. With the help of an outside firm, Penny was also able to confirm the source of the negative online content—it originated from the former marketing manager's home computer, as suspected—and have it removed, with the help of a letter from her attorney threatening legal action.

Pitfalls

Below are several of the most common pitfalls we have observed related to exit in family firms.

Rushing or avoiding exit. Because exit is so uncomfortable, it is tempting to put if off—the phenomenon of the "overstayed welcome" discussed earlier—or to rush through it, for both the employer and the employee. Both of these are suboptimal, because they can result in wasted resources and negative emotions. Taking a more thoughtful, systematic approach to exit, including the components discussed here, can help you handle it in a more optimal way for all parties.

Not following your systems. The mere presence of a good exit system does not ensure it will be used. Again, due to the complexity and ambiguity of exit situations, many people will take shortcuts (rushing), fail to take advantage of the system (avoiding), or misuse it in some way. This may be more likely in a culture with lower emphasis on accountability. So aim not only to develop an exit system but to ensure that the organization understands its components and value. HR can be a valuable partner on both counts.

Forgetting the fine print. If there is one thing people avoid more than dealing with exits, it is dealing with legal matters. That makes the legal component of exits especially challenging for family firms, including the noncompete, nondisclosure, and other issues discussed earlier. Failure to attend to these aspects can result in a range of consequences from minor hassles to major reputation-damaging events. We recommend "enlarging" the fine print related to exits: make it *big* print, so everyone is aware of the legal ramifications of leaving the firm, ideally before they begin the process to depart. Again, HR can and should play a critical role in this area.

Things to Remember

Here are the key points we made in this chapter about the important but often overlooked or avoided topic of exit in the family business.

- It is critical for family firms to manage exits well because this is linked closely to trust and relationship building. Exits have a huge impact on the entire system, such that a departure from one circle—in this chapter, the business circle—can become a departure from multiple circles (i.e., family and ownership). Exits influence perceptions of the importance of performance within the firm (less care with exit management implies less care for performance standards).
- We view exit as a *transition* process for the business and the departing individual, rather than a time-limited event. This means developing a conscious, thoughtful system that will help you manage exits strategically, rather than avoiding them or rushing them.

- The two kinds of exit are *voluntary* (such as to seek education, a new job, or retirement) and *involuntary* (due to poor competence or chemistry, downsizing, or other factors). Best practices related to any type of exit include considering limiting the number of times an employee can depart/re-enter the business, avoiding overstayed welcomes, and discussing the "undiscussables" such as underperformance.
- Components of a strategic exit management system include those implemented before, during, and after the exit, with a sample of best practices for each below:
  - *Before the exit:* Develop a transition plan including who will cover for the departing person in the short and long term (this is important for planned and unplanned departures); communicate thoroughly with the departing person and a broader audience; pay close attention to legal issues, including noncompetes.
  - *During the exit:* Conduct exit interviews to understand the departing employee's reasons for leaving and related implications for improvement; establish outplacement services to help people find their next opportunity; celebrate the departing employee, especially if they have been with the firm for a long period as a valued contributor.
  - *After the exit:* Keep informal track of former employee destinations, especially those with whom there is value in maintaining some contact as potential partners, customers, or even future (re-entering) employees; develop a clear re-entry policy and communicate this throughout the firm.
- Common pitfalls associated with exits include rushing or avoiding departures, failing to follow the exit management systems you have developed (because of the sensitivity and complexity of exit), and forgetting to attend to the "fine print" (legal matters).

Parting Words

In the previous chapters we provided an array of frameworks, tools, and tips for taking a strategic approach to HR in your family business. We have explored the important contribution of HR in family businesses, beginning with the firm's culture and continuing through every stage of the HR lifecycle, from recruiting to development to exit. Here, in this final chapter, we want to help you understand how to move from ideas to action most effectively. We will provide guidance on how HR can interface with the governance forums within a family firm and help manage a range of special circumstances the business may face. We also offer some tips for enhancing HR's capabilities in whatever form this function takes in your organization.

Remember that our approach involves viewing HR as an *internal partner* rather than as a "policing" function, as a *highly strategic service* instead of a transactional manager, and as a *true value generator* rather than merely a cost center. With that philosophy in mind, let us talk about some of the ways you can begin to put the ideas we have offered into action.

Making It Work

Our work with hundreds of family businesses makes clear that change is never easy, no matter what your firm's specific size or shape. Families successfully lead and grow their firms for decades, relying upon the original values and principles of the founding generation. Resistance to change is not just a rule of physics (inertia, that is), but a very real phenomenon for the families we have helped and observed. Arming yourself with the tips below can help you begin to influence and reshape your HR practices.

Start small, but start somewhere. Given the sea of tips about family business practices out there—on everything from governance to succession—it is easy to drown. Just between the covers of this book are more practical ideas for making HR effective than most companies could realistically consider in a year. So where do you start? We advocate starting small, in an area that clearly needs attention, ideally one in which you can generate some success with relative ease. Quick wins are an important, powerful factor in generating momentum and increased support for future efforts, as discussed more below. If the general mood in the business is not positive, it may be time to revisit cultural issues, perhaps starting with the Family Values Exercise presented in the "Culture" chapter. If new hires have not been working out well, then the "Recruiting" and "Selection" chapters offer tips for improvement. Sure, you could put together an HR task force and pursue a highly strategic approach that maps out your current set of HR issues comprehensively and sets a multiyear plan of attack. There is nothing wrong with that tack, and it would work for some firms. But it might make others feel overwhelmed. We would rather you start somewhere than not at all, and small steps can be the best response to inertia.

Think top down. We have emphasized throughout the book that change will not happen without genuine support from the leadership team, which includes family owners and top executives. It is ideal when top leadership enlists HR as a strategic partner to address human resources "hot spots" and directs HR to get involved with key efforts that will strengthen corporate culture, recruiting, onboarding, or any of the areas covered in prior chapters. In order for HR to make its full potential contribution to organizational excellence, it needs clear support and direction from senior management. The first step may be as simple as getting top leaders to suggest a high-priority, quick-win initiative, as discussed next.

Think bottom up. Not all meaningful action starts from the top. You can drive results by starting with a small but important change to your HR practices, as mentioned earlier. A quick win in a strategically important area—tying selection more closely to the business's values, for example—can create buy-in by linking HR's role and impact more directly to operational priorities (in this case, hiring the best people for the job more effectively). And small changes lead naturally to larger-scale ones, thus serving multiple ends. So think carefully about a *grassroots-level* change you can implement, and then move into execution mode. The "Aim for Small Wins" Box has specific ideas to get you started.

Aim for Small Wins

Here are some ideas to get you started thinking about small HR wins in your organization, especially those that reinforce your culture:

- Ask good thought-starter questions, such as "What do we value here and how do we reward it?"
- Honor key strengths of your existing culture by leaving a coffee gift card on an employee's desk with a thank-you note related to how they exemplify a core firm value (e.g., quality, customer service, respect, hard work).
- Bring in experts to train managers on good customer service (managers should be your role models).
- Tell stories of employee behavior that is consistent with the company's core values. For example, one family business in health care frequently tells the story of an employee who drove all night to deliver a vital medical product to a customer!

Start from your strengths. Like most family firms, you may have strengths you do not even realize. One of the most powerful is *values.* Family businesses are typically built on long-standing values that inform their culture and practices. So we often encourage families looking to enhance HR practices to harness their values in service of change. That might mean deploying values more explicitly in hiring or development, as discussed in the "Selection" and "Development" chapters, respectively. At the same time, some businesses (for example, manufacturers) may be especially strong at developing standardized processes. This strength can be applied to HR practices by making them more systematic and repeatable, again based on principles in this book. The idea is that working from a strength is often an easier way to start than the alternative.

Get everyone on board. Who should lead the process of transforming HR in your business? Ideally, a combination of HR leaders, other executives, and if possible family members should provide leadership from the top. Some firms, especially smaller ones, do not even have a formal HR group, so making changes to HR practices is by definition the responsibility of all managers. For example, at Canada's Kal Tire (discussed in detail in the "Culture" chapter), HR is seen as the responsibility of every store manager. When a formal, centralized HR organization exists, it can serve in a "leading support" role, spearheading change through a collaborative process. We believe firmly that while HR can serve as the champion of the ideas in this book, a team approach that includes participation of all key groups will lead to the best results.

Remember that measurement matters. Do not forget to gauge progress on any number of dimensions. Many firms get excited about making changes to their HR systems but overlook the need to measure the *impact* of initiatives. However, the more process-focused nature of HR functions can make it challenging to measure improvement. The assessment tools described in the "Culture" chapter can help you understand general satisfaction levels and other measures in your firm; data from performance reviews (discussed in the "Development" chapter) can highlight employee capabilities and advancement rates; and exit interviews (as discussed in the "Exit" chapter) can point to both positive and negative issues across the organization. And there is a wide range of other tools you can use—off-the-shelf, customized, or brought in by third parties—to gauge progress, or lack thereof. The most important thing is to do it.

HR and Governance

Governance is a tricky area for family firms, in terms of both the business and the family. Because of challenges related to understanding the structures and processes that will best fit a given business at a given time, and how to implement these, many firms procrastinate or avoid addressing the need for governance structures.[1] However, good governance is critical for continued family firm success, and HR can help. Here we highlight key points of intersection between HR and family firm governance that can create value for the business.

First, HR can serve a key role in facilitating *communication*. For example, if a firm has a family council, HR can help establish and maintain a connection between the family council and the company, better integrating the family's views and voice into the business's vision and strategy. Specifically, HR executives might help support family council education initiatives or plan a family retreat at which board members may participate in part of the session. Similarly, HR can have a clear role in *succession planning* and *family engagement*, working with the family council to prepare the next generation for roles in the business or governance arenas through educational opportunities (such as leadership or internship programs, as discussed in the "Recruiting" chapter), along with other measures. HR can also work closely with the executive team and the family on *policy setting*, such as that related to family employment and compensation.

We have emphasized the importance of *culture* in the family business as "the water the fish swim in"—or the context that influences all systems, processes, and interactions. As such, it is important for HR and governance bodies to work together in creating and supporting a healthy culture, ideally one based on identified values. That can mean working together to ensure the business invests in and consciously builds its culture on an ongoing basis, using suggestions laid out in the "Culture" chapter. HR can and should play a central role in reinforcing a strong, values-based culture, in support of efforts of the board, family, and ownership councils.

HR and Special Circumstances

HR can also play a role in managing special circumstances within the business and/or family that may not fit neatly into the HR lifecycle or cultural issues discussed earlier in the book. Such circumstances and issues include

- movement from a family CEO to a nonfamily chief executive;
- the death of a family member (whether that person works within the family enterprise or not);
- family conflicts (including divorce, estrangement, infidelity);

- substance abuse issues; and
- crime/legal issues (including sexual harassment)

It is best *not* to consider the involvement of HR in these and other special circumstances only when they arise, but rather to have some overarching criteria in place already to guide the decision to involve HR. For example, some family firms establish an expectation that HR gets involved with any issue that affects the *business* significantly, whether it occurs inside or outside the business. Even if HR is not centrally involved in a specific issue, it can play an important role as a sounding board and/or communication facilitator, offering perspective not only on reputational implications of such matters but also on potential solutions. HR can also serve to raise awareness of and enforce policies related to drug testing, sexual harassment, and other areas, ensuring the rules are in place and that they are being followed.

HR can develop guiding principles to use in helping the business make decisions related to particular issues or challenges, including special circumstances. One such set of guiding principles appears in the "Four-Way Test for Ethical Behavior" Box. HR, with the help of other leaders within the firm, can develop the principles that make sense for the business that houses it and the family that owns it.

A Four-Way Test for Ethical Behavior

The worldwide service organization Rotary International has developed a "Four-Way Test" to help its members behave ethically and in one another's best interests.[2] The guiding principles the organization uses can serve as a foundation or inspiration for HR to use in helping the business make decisions and form solutions, especially for tricky special circumstances like those discussed above.

Of the things we think, say, or do,

1. is it the TRUTH?
2. is it FAIR to all concerned?
3. will it build GOODWILL and BETTER FRIENDSHIPS?
4. will it be BENEFICIAL to all concerned?

Enhancing HR's Capabilities

There are multiple ways in which HR can boost its capabilities related to family business (beyond reading this book!). We have identified three routes HR professionals and other managers can take to enhance their family business skills.

Formal approaches. Joining professional organizations, earning certifications, going to workshops and seminars, and engaging consultants are all routes to boosting capability. Canada offers the Certified Human Resources Professional (CHRP) designation, for example, to HR professionals who go through a structured training and testing program—the focus is broader than family business, but may still be of value.[3] Similarly, the Family Business Network brings professionals from family businesses worldwide together for conferences, workshops, and webinars.[4] Multiple consultancies (including ours, the Family Business Consulting Group) also offer advisory services, workshops, and other resources to boost HR capabilities in family business. The "A Sample of Family Business Resources" Box presents some well-known organizations that focus on supporting family firms.

A Start on Family Business Resources

- Canadian Association of Family Enterprise (CAFÉ Canada)
- Family Business Network
- Family Firm Institute
- Family Office Exchange (FOX)
- Institute for Family Enterprise Advisors
- Transitions West and Transitions East Conferences
- University-based Family Business Centers (such as the one at Northwestern University's Kellogg School of Management and the University of British Columbia's Sauder's School of Business [Business Families Centre])

Informal approaches. Reading books like this one is an informal approach to boosting your HR capabilities, and so is talking to HR

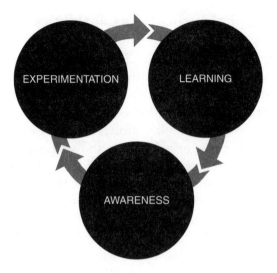

Figure 9.1   A cycle of experimentation, learning, and awareness.

and other professionals within family business, to understand their experience and insights. We are always impressed by the amount of "peer-to-peer" learning that takes place between family businesses; it is hard to duplicate the value of speaking from experience. As such, we encourage you to seek out other family businesses—especially those that may already have dealt with some of the issues you face— and talk to them about their HR challenges and the solutions they have developed. You may be surprised by how much you can learn.

The cycle of self-awareness and experimentation. This last category combines elements of the first two into the idea that you can use everything you learn to inform your sense of your current capabilities, and to try new things in your business. It may be something as simple as a new interview questionnaire for employee candidates (perhaps one based on foundational business values) or something as comprehensive as an overhaul of your performance management system. Learning is doing, and vice versa. So learn what you can from formal and informal routes, and then put your new knowledge into action, learning more as you go, as suggested by the visual in Figure 9.1.

Aim for Constant Evolution

Family business is a key contributor to the global economy, society, and culture, as we highlighted in the introduction. And HR systems are fundamental to the success of family firms, especially when HR is viewed as a strategic partner and value generator. It is critical to make your HR systems the best they can be, by taking an active, conscious approach built on the ideas here.

That said, you cannot get everything right the first time you seek to transform any HR system or process. You *will not* get everything right the first time. And even if you get something right, the business/family circumstances will change at some point, requiring revisiting and revising whatever it is. That is all part of our theme of *constant evolution*, an idea we encourage you to embrace. Things change. The goal is to help them change for the better.

So take a good, close look at the many moving parts of your firm's HR systems and processes, and take the first steps, however small, toward making them the best they can be.

Things to Remember

Here are the main points we have made in this chapter.

- While change is never easy, several tips can help you work toward improving your HR systems and processes: starting small, gaining early support of the leadership team, looking for opportunities for small wins, and leveraging strengths related to multiple aspects of the business, among others.
- HR is linked to the governance of your firm through its roles in communication—such as helping to connect a family council or similar governance body with the broader business—and in championing the firm's culture among all stakeholders.
- The HR function also plays a role in managing special circumstances, such as the death of a family member, family conflicts, and crime/legal issues. Here, it is best to have criteria in place for understanding when HR should have a leadership or support role, such as whether the issue in question affects the business significantly.
- Your firm's HR capabilities can be enhanced by both formal (such as seminars and certifications) and informal (such as books and peer-to-peer learning) resources, as part of an ongoing cycle of self-awareness, experimentation, and learning—reflecting the broader theme of constant evolution.

Notes

1 Introduction

1. Marcia Conner, "Now that People Finally Matter to Businesses, HR Is the Next Big Thing," *Fast Company*, September 30, 2011, http://www.fastcompany.com/1783518/now-people-finally-matter-businesses-hr-next-big-thing (accessed March 9, 2015).
2. As noted in Kevin Kruse, "Employee Engagement: The Wonder Drug in Customer Satisfaction," *Forbes*, January 7, 2014, http://www.forbes.com/sites/kevinkruse/2014/01/07/employee-engagement-the-wonder-drug-for-customer-satisfaction/ (accessed April 12, 2015).
3. R. Anderson and D. Reeb, "Founding Family Ownership and Firm Performance: Evidence from the S&P 500," *Journal of Finance*, Vol. 58, No. 3 (2003): 1308–1328.
4. Antonio Spizzirri and Matt Fullbrook, "The Impact of Family Control on the Share Price Performance of Large Canadian Publicly-Listed Firms from 1998 to 2012," Clarkson Centre for Board Effectiveness Report, June 2013.
5. Nicolas Kachaner, George Stalk, and Alain Bloch, "What You Can Learn from Family Business," *Harvard Business Review*, November 2012, https://hbr.org/2012/11/what-you-can-learn-from-family-business.
6. John B. Bingham, W. Gibb Dyer Jr., Isaac Smith, and Gregory L. Adams, "A Stakeholder Identity Orientation Approach to Corporate Social Performance in Family Firms," *Journal of Business Ethics*, Vol. 99, No. 4 (2011): 565–585.
7. See, for example, David Beatty and Matt Fullbrook, "The Upside of Family Ties," *Rotman Magazine*, Fall 2013, 59–63.
8. Ellie Filler and Dave Ulrich, "Why Chief Human Resources Officers Make Great CEOs," *Harvard Business Review*, December 2014, https://hbr.org/2014/12/why-chief-human-resources-officers-make-great-ceos?utm_campaign=Socialflow&utm_source=Socialflow&utm_medium=Tweet (accessed March 12, 2015).

9. Sources for elements of our definitions include Craig E. Aronoff, Stephen L. McClure, and John L. Ward, *Family Business Ownership: How To Be an Effective Shareholder* (New York: Palgrave Macmillan, 2010); Luis R. Gomez-Mejia, Martin Larraza-Kintana, and Marianna Makri, "The Determinants of Executive Compensation in Family-Controlled Public Corporations," *Academy of Management Journal*, Vol. 46, No. 2 (2003): 226–237; Pramodita Sharma, James Chrisman, and Jesse Chua, "Strategic Management of the Family Business: Past Research and Future Challenges," *Family Business Review*, 1997, Vol. 10, No. 1 (1997): 1–35.

10. We recognize that many companies now call their employees "associates" or "coworkers" to indicate a stronger sense of collegiality or to emphasize a flat organization. Although we use the more traditional term "employee" for expedience, we appreciate the power and symbolism of this growing alternative terminology.

11. For much more on how to understand and handle paradox in family business, see Amy Schuman, Stacy Stutz, and John L. Ward, *Family Business as Paradox* (New York: Palgrave Macmillan, 2010).

2   Our Model

1. Randel Carlock and John L. Ward, *Strategic Planning for the Family and Business* (New York: Palgrave, 2001).

2. Carlock and Ward, *Strategic Planning*.

3. For a good summary of parallel planning and its four dimensions, see Otis Baskin, "Developing a Winning Strategy for the Family and the Business," *The Family Business Advisor* (FBCG newsletter), March 2012, http://archive.constantcontact.com/fs093/1100669808564 /archive/1109275405858.html (accessed March 31, 2015).

4. Renato Tagiuri and John Davis, "Bivalent Attributes of a Family Firm," *Family Business Review*, Vol. 9, No. 2 (1996): 199–208.

5. For more on systems thinking, see Peter Senge, *The Fifth Discipline* (New York: Doubleday, 1990).

3   Culture

1. Kal Tire, "Our Aims," Company website, http://info.kaltire.com/about-us/aims (accessed February 17, 2015).

2. As quoted in many sources, including Adam Levin, "Post-Target Data Security: Culture Eats Strategy for Breakfast," *Forbes*, June 12, 2014,

http://www.forbes.com/sites/adamlevin/2014/06/12/post-target-data
-security-culture-eats-strategy-for-breakfast/ (accessed December 12,
2014).

3. See, for example, E. H. Schein, *Organizational Culture and Leadership:
   A Dynamic View* (San Francisco: Jossey-Bass, 1985).
4. This idea was forwarded in early business books on corporate culture,
   including T. E. Deal and A. A. Kennedy, *Corporate Cultures* ([Reading,
   Mass] Addison-Wesley, 1982).
5. See, for example, John L. Ward, "Family Values for Competitive
   Advantage," *Campden Family Business*, March 1, 2005, http://www.
   campdenfb.com/article/family-values-competitive-advantage
   (accessed August 7, 2014).
6. Daniel Denison, Colleen Lief, and John L. Ward, "Culture in Family-
   Owned Enterprises: Recognizing and Leveraging Unique Strengths,"
   Family Business Review, Vol. 17 (2004): 61.
7. Ward, "Family Values for Competitive Advantage."
8. Alexandra Sharpe, "Aligning Family and Business Values," *Tharawat
   Magazine*, October 12, 2012, pp. 16–19.
9. See, for example, Geil Browning, "The Collaboration Effect: How
   Millennials Are Impacting Leadership," *Inc.*, October 9, 2014, http://
   www.inc.com/geil-browning/the-collaboration-effect-how-millenni-
   als-are-impacting-leadership.html (accessed December 16, 2014).
10. For more on interactions among generational cohorts in family busi-
    ness, see Mark Green, *Inside the Multi-generational Family Business*
    (New York: Palgrave-Macmillan, 2011).
11. As quoted in Eric Jackson, "The Top 8 Reasons Your Best People Are
    About to Quit," *Forbes*, May 11, 2014, http://www.forbes.com/sites
    /ericjackson/2014/05/11/the-top-8-reasons-your-best-people-are
    -about-to-quit-and-how-you-can-keep-them/ (accessed February 17,
    2015).
12. Marci Koblenz and Alice Campbell, *A New Paradigm: The Work and
    Life Pyramid of Needs* (Deerfield, IL: Baxter Healthcare, 1997).
13. Kim Cameron and Robert Quinn, *Diagnosing and Changing Organiza-
    tional Culture*, 3rd edition (San Francisco: Jossey-Bass, 2011).
14. Rachel Emma Silverman, "Are You Happy at Work? Bosses Push Week-
    ly Polls," *Wall Street Journal*, December 2, 2014, http://www.wsj.com
    /articles/more-bosses-use-short-frequent-polls-to-measure-morale
    -1417550446 (accessed December 18, 2014).
15. For an example of a card-sort approach, see Dennis Jaffe and Cynthia
    Scott, "How to Link Personal Values to Team Values," dennisjaffe.com,
    http://dennisjaffe.com/adminpanel/uploads/documents/1307423812
    ASTDValuesArticle.pdf (accessed December 22, 2014).

16. Andrew Carton, Chad Murphy, and Jonathan Clark, "A Blurry Vision of the Future: How Leader Rhetoric about Ultimate Goals Influences Performance," *Academy of Management Journal*, Vol. 57, No. 6 (2014): 1544–1570.

17. The basis for the model is described in Daniel Denison, *Corporate Culture and Organizational Effectiveness* (New York: Wiley, 1990).

18. Randel S. Carlock and John L. Ward, *Strategic Planning for the Family Business: Parallel Planning to Unite the Family and the Business* (New York: Palgrave Macmillan, 2001).

19. For more on Human Synergistics, see www.humansynergistics.com.

20. For more on Polarity Partnerships, see www.polaritypartnerships.com.

21. W. Gibb Dyer, Jr., "Culture and Continuity in Family Firms," *Family Business Review*, Vol.1, No. 1 (1988): 18–24.

22. Kim Cameron and Robert Quinn, *Diagnosing and Changing Organizational Culture,* 3rd edition (San Francisco: Jossey-Bass, 2011).

23. For more about Radio Flyer's history, see Reshma Yaqub, "Backstory: Radio Flyer," *Inc.*, October 30, 2012, http://www.inc.com/magazine/201211/reshma-memon-yaqub/backstory-radio-flyer.html (accessed December 18, 2014).

24. See, for example, Leonard Johnson and Alan Frohman, "Identifying and Closing the Gap in the Middle of Organizations," *Academy of Management Executive*, Vol. 3, No. 2 (1983): 107.

4 Recruiting

1. See, for example Erin White, "Manager Shortage Spurs Small Firms to Grow Their Own," *Wall Street Journal Online*, February 5, 2007, http://online.wsj.com/news/articles/SB117063558473797776 (accessed June 17, 2014).

2. As cited in Elena Bajic, "How to Avoid Becoming a Hiring Mistake," *Forbes*, April 15, 2014, http://www.forbes.com/sites/elenabajic/2014/04/15/how-to-avoid-becoming-a-hiring-mistake/ (accessed June 23, 2014).

3. Family Owned Business Institute, Family Owned Business Survey 2014, http://issuu.com/neumagazine/docs/annual_report1/0 (accessed October 30, 2014).

4. See, for example, Acacia Squires, "The 'Bitter' Tale of the Budweiser Family," *The Salt*, NPR, December 22, 2012, http://www.npr.org/blogs/thesalt/2012/12/22/166493220/the-bitter-tale-of-the-budweiser-family (accessed August 13, 2014).

5. Roy Williams and Vic Preisser, *Preparing Heirs: Five Steps to a Successful Transition of Family Wealth and Values* (San Francisco: Robert Reed, 2010).

6. See, for example, George Stalk and Henry Foley, "Avoid the Traps That Can Destroy Family Businesses," *Harvard Business Review*, January-February 2012, http://hbr.org/2012/01/avoid-the-traps-that-can-destroy-family-businesses/ar/1 (accessed October 30, 2014).

7. As noted in Rachel Breitman and Del Jones, "Should Kids Be Left Fortunes, Or Left Out?" *USA Today*, July 26, 2006, http://usatoday30.usatoday.com/money/2006-07-25-heirs-usat_x.htm (accessed June 17, 2014).

8. Kemmons Wilson Family Foundation webpage, http://kwilson.com/wilsonfoundation/ (accessed April 20, 2015).

9. Claudio Fernandez Araoz, "21st Century Talent Spotting," *Harvard Business Review*, June 2014, 46–56.

10. Craig E. Aronoff and John L. Ward, *More Than Family: Non-Family Executives in the Family Business* (New York: Palgrave Macmillan, 2011).

11. For more on Forum Groups, see www.vistage.com, www.mackayceoforums.com, www.tec-canada.com; for more on YPO, see www.ypo.org.

12. For more on the NACD, see www.nacdonline.org; for more on the Institute of Corporate Directors, see www.icd.ca.

13. As cited in "8 Keys to Better Networking," Salary.com, http://www.salary.com/8-keys-to-better-networking/ (accessed June 17, 2014).

14. Family Owned Business Institute, Family Owned Business Survey 2014, http://issuu.com/neumagazine/docs/annual_report1/0 (accessed October 30, 2014).

15. Aronoff and Ward, *More Than Family.*.

16. Aronoff and Ward, *More Than Family.*

17. Jim Collins, *Good to Great* (New York: HarperBusiness, 2001).

5   Selection

1. As cited in Elena Bajic, "How to Avoid Becoming a Hiring Mistake," *Forbes*, April 15, 2014, http://www.forbes.com/sites/elenabajic/2014/04/15/how-to-avoid-becoming-a-hiring-mistake/ (accessed June 23, 2014)

2. Will Wei, "Tony Hsieh: Bad Hires Have Cost Zappos Over $100 Million," BusinessInsider.com, October 25, 2010, http://www.businessinsider.com/tony-hsieh-making-the-right-hires-2010–10#ixzz38J4Ym0DM (accessed July 23, 2014).

3. See, for example, Thomas Zellweger, "Risk, Return and Value in the Family Firm," Thesis, University of St. Gallen, 2006, https://www.alexandria.unisg.ch/publications/28817 (accessed August 22, 2014). Note, however, that risk aversion is not a *universal* trait among family firms. We have seen several cases of families who are very willing to take large risks, including as related to selection. Sometimes these hiring bets pay off well, while other times they break the bank.

4. Gary Hamel, "W.L. Gore: Lessons from a Management Revolutionary," *Wall Street Journal* (blog), March 18, 2010, http://blogs.wsj.com/management/2010/03/18/wl-gore-lessons-from-a-management-revolutionary/ (accessed August 25, 2014).

5. For more on the Hogan Personality Inventory, see www.hoganassessments.com (accessed July 23, 2014).

6. For more on the MBTI and its applications, see resources available through the Myers & Briggs Foundation, http://www.myersbriggs.org/my-mbti-personality-type/mbti-basics/ (accessed July 23, 2014).

7. Therese Macan, "The Employment Interview: A Review of Current Studies and Directions for Future Research," *Human Resource Management Review*, Vol. 19, No. 3 (2009): 203–218.

8. Macan, "The Employment Interview."

9. For more on DDI, see http://www.ddiworld.com/.

10. For the 2014 version of Fuqua's question, see http://www.fuqua.duke.edu/daytime-mba/admissions/application-instructions/ (accessed July 24, 2014).

11. See. for example, Thomas M. Zellweger, Kimberly A. Eddleston, and Franz W. Kellermanns, "Exploring the Concept of Familiness: Introducing Family Firm Identity," *Journal of Family Business Strategy* Vol. 1 (2010): 54–63.

12. See, for example, Jill Hamburg Coplan, "How Positive Psychology Can Boost Your Business," *BusinessWeek*, February 12, 2009, http://www.businessweek.com/stories/2009-02-12/how-positive-psychology-can-boost-your-business (accessed July 24, 2014).

6 Onboarding

1. As quoted by Anne-Marie Slaughter, "Yes, You Can: Sheryl Sandberg's *Lean In*," *New York Times*, March 7, 2013, http://www.nytimes.com/2013/03/10/books/review/sheryl-sandbergs-lean-in.html?pagewanted=all&_r=0 (accessed July 29, 2014); note that Slaughter was discussing Princeton University's finding that how well female undergraduates rose to early leadership opportunities

predicted whether they received future such opportunities—a topic related to that of employee onboarding.

2. See, for example, "The Importance of Onboarding," *Inc.*, April 25, 2013, http://www.inc.com/thebuildnetwork/the-importance-of -onboarding.html (accessed July 29, 2014).

3. As cited in George Bradt, "Executive Onboarding: The Key to Accelerating Success and Reducing Risk in a New Job," *Forbes*, February 15, 2012, http://www.forbes.com/sites/georgebradt/2012/02/15/ executive-onboarding-the-key-to-accelerating-success-and-reducing -risk-in-a-new-job/ (accessed July 29, 2014).

4. Human Capital Institute, "Best Practices for Onboarding: Assuring Successful Assimilation" (White Paper), April 2011, http://www.scribd .com/doc/60446897/DBM-Best-Practices-for-Onboarding#scribd (accessed February 7, 2015).

5. See, for example, The Motley Fool employee policies page, http://the-foolrules.com/motley-fool/policies (accessed November 19, 2014).

6. Michael Watkins, *The First 90 Days* (Cambridge, MA: Harvard Business School Press, 2003).

7. Boris Groysberg, Ashish Nanda, and Nitin Nohria, "The Risky Business of Hiring Stars," *Harvard Business Review*, May 2004, https:// hbr.org/2004/05/the-risky-business-of-hiring-stars/ar/1 (accessed November 19, 2014).

7   Development

1. As cited in Andy Teng, "Making the Business Case for HR: Talent Management Aids Earnings," *HR Today*, May 10, 2007, http://www .hrotoday.com/news/talent-acquisition/making-the-business-case -for-hr-talent-management-aids-earnings/ (accessed March 26, 2015).

2. See, for example, Robin Lowe and Sue Marriott, *Enterprise: Entrepreneurship and Innovation* (London: Routledge, 2012).

3. For more on the concept and features of a learning organization, see Peter Senge, *The Fifth Discipline: The Art and Practice of the Learning Organization* (New York: Doubleday, 2006).

4. Stephen Hurley, "As We Speak: The Difference Between a Job and a Role," Blog post, stephenhurley.ca, March 21, 2013, http://www .stephenhurley.ca/as-we-speak-the-difference-between-job-and -role/ (accessed March 23, 2015).

5. For much more thinking on compensation in family business, for example, see Craig Aronoff, Stephen McClure, and John L. Ward, *Compensation in Family Business* (New York: Palgrave Macmillan, 2010).

6. For more on managing succession in family business, see Amy Schuman, *Nurturing the Talent to Nurture the Legacy: Career Development in the Family Business* (New York: Palgrave Macmillan, 2010) and Aronoff, McClure, and Ward, *Family Business Succession.*

7. John L. Ward, *Keeping the Family Business Healthy* (New York: Palgrave Macmillan, 2010).

8. Stephen P. Miller, "Developing Next-Generation Leaders in Family Business," The Family Business Advisor (newsletter of The Family Business Consulting Group).

9. For much more on approaches to nonfamily executives in the family business, see Craig E. Aronoff and John L. Ward, *More than Family: Non-family Executives in the Family Business* (New York: Palgrave Macmillan, 2011).

10. Two of us have served as coaches for the Kellogg-based family business workshops. For more on the school's offerings in this area, see the Kellogg Center for Family Enterprises website, http://www.kellogg .northwestern.edu/execed/programs/fambiz.aspx (accessed March 25, 2013).

11. Amazon search for keyword "business" in "Books" category, http://www.amazon.com/s/ref=nb_sb_noss_1?url=search-alias% 3Dstripbooks&field-keywords=business (accessed March 25, 2015).

12. For more about the Association for Talent Development, see their website: www.astd.com.

13. Jack Zenger and Joseph Folkman, "Your Employees Want the Negative Feedback You Hate to Give," *Harvard Business Review,* January 15, 2014, https://hbr.org/2014/01/your-employees-want-the-negative -feedback-you-hate-to-give/ (accessed March 25, 2015).

14. Eric Jackson, "The 7 Reasons Why 360-Degree Feedback Programs Fail," *Forbes,* August 17, 2012, http://www.forbes.com/sites /ericjackson/2012/08/17/the-7-reasons-why-360-degree-feedback -programs-fail/ (accessed March 23, 2015).

8   Exit

1. As cited in Alan Hall, "I'm Outta Here: Why 2 Million Americans Quit Every Month," *Forbes,* March 11, 2013, http://www.forbes.com/sites /alanhall/2013/03/11/im-outta-here-why-2-million-americans-quit -every-month-and-5-steps-to-turn-the-epidemic-around/ (accessed January 30, 2015).

2. Linda Nguyen, "More Canadians Leaving Their Jobs after Just Two Years," *The Globe and Mail,* April 25, 2014, http://www.theglo

beandmail.com/report-on-business/careers/career-advice/more
-canadians-leaving-their-jobs-after-just-two-years-poll/arti-
cle18051842/ (accessed April 10, 2015).

3. S. Brown, G. Garino, and C. Martin, "Firm Performance and Labour
Turnover: Evidence from the 2004 Workplace Employee Relations
Survey," *Economic Modeling*, Vol. 26 (2009): 689–695.

4. See, for example, Donna DeZube, "Use the Exit Interview to Reduce
Employee Turnover," Monster.com, http://hiring.monster.com/hr
/hr-best-practices/small-business/conducting-an-interview/exit
-interview.aspx (accessed January 30, 2015).

5. The 3-Circle model first appeared in Renato Tagiuri and John Davis,
"Bivalent Attributes of the Family Firm," *Family Business Review*, Vol
9, no. 2. (1996): 199–208.

6. While an individual may technically exit the business, ownership, and/
or the family, this chapter will focus on exit from the business/employ-
ment, as that tends to be the main focus of management and the HR
function. In fact, our recommendations for an exit system are aimed
at ensuring family employees who choose to depart their business
positions with the firm do not depart their other role as active family
members and/or shareholders.

7. Trapeze analogy and figure for exits from William Bridges, *Managing
Transitions: Making Sense of Life's Changes* (Cambridge, MA, Da Capo
Books, 2009).

8. For a discussion of how inertia applies to everything from fitness to
401(k) retirement account choices, see Richard Thaler and Cass Sun-
stein, *Nudge: Improving Decisions about Health, Wealth, and Happiness*
(New Haven, CT: Yale University Press, 2008).

9. For an extensive discussion of understanding and managing tran-
sitions including exits, see William Bridges and Susan Bridges,
Managing Transitions: Making the Most of Change (Philadelpha: Da
Capo Lifelong Books, 2009).

10. Allison Rimm and Celia Brown, "Know When to Fire Someone," *Harvard Business Review*, January 7, 2015, https://hbr.org/2015/01/know-
ing-when-to-fire-someone/ (accessed February 10, 2015).

11. Josh Moss, "The Best Bourbon You'll Never Taste," *Louisville Magazine*, July 2013, 67.

12. See, for example, David Rock, "The Neuroscience of Leadership," *Psychology Today*, March 10, 2011, https://www.psychologytoday.com
/blog/your-brain-work/201103/the-neuroscience-leadership (accessed
February 9, 2015).

13. Jeffrey Sonnenfeld and Padraic Spence, "The Parting Patriarch of a
Family Firm," *Family Business Review*, Vol. 2, No. 4(1989): 355–375.

14. There are many options for creating a personal keepsake gift for departing employees. These range from creating a simple do-it -yourself picture scrapbook to hiring a specialty company to interview employees and edit the content into a video with special effects.

9   Parting Words

1. For example, a Deloitte study shows that 28% of family businesses have no formal board of directors; Deloitte, "Perspectives on Family-Owned Businesses: Governance and Succession," 2013, http://www.corpgov.deloitte.com/binary/com.epicentric.content-management.servlet.ContentDeliveryServlet/CanEng/Documents/Private%20Companies/Corporate%20Governance/Family-ownedBusinessReport-v9.pdf (accessed March 3, 2015).
2. Rotary International, "Guiding Principles: The Four-Way Test," https://www.rotary.org/myrotary/en/learning-reference/about-rotary/guiding-principles (accessed March 3, 2015).
3. For more on the CHRP designation, see www.chrp.ca.
4. For more on the Family Business Network see http://fbn-na.org/ (North American chapter) or http://fbn-i.org (international chapter).

Index

giving performance feedback, 141
transparency, 69

undiscussables, 137, 176, 178, 180,
    186, 189

values, 17–22, 24–5, 37, 43, 52, 54, 61
    see also family values exercise
Van Winkle, Pappy, 180
Vincent, Jeff, 147
Vistage, 74
voluntary exits
    explained, 172
    learning from, 174–5
    limiting number of times for
        entering and exiting, 174

negative reasons for, 173–5
not taking personally, 173–4
positive reasons for, 173
suggestions for dealing with, 173–5
see also exits; involuntary exits

W.L. Gore and Associates, 87–8
Ward, John L., 16, 34, 44, 51–2,
    75, 144
Watkins, Michael, 122
Wilson, Kemmons, 71

Young Presidents' Organization
    (YPO), 74

Zappos, 82

ADDITIONAL BESTSELLING BOOKS FOR YOUR FAMILY BUSINESS LIBRARY

$23.00
978-0-230-11100-4

$23.00
978-0-230-11106-6

$23.00
978-0-230-11108-0

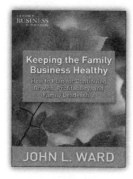

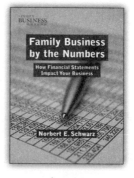

$50.00
978-0-230-11121-9

$45.00
978-0-230-11123-3

"Each Family Business Leadership publication is packed cover-to-cover with expert guidance, solid information and ideas that work."

—Alan Campbell, CFO, Campbell Motel Properties, Inc., Brea, CA

"While each volume contains helpful 'solutions' to the issues it covers, it is the guidance on how to tackle the process of addressing the different issues, and the emphasis on the benefits which can stem from the process itself, which make the Family Business publications of unique value to everyone involved in a family business—not just the owners."

—David Grant, Director (retired), William Grant & Sons Ltd. (distillers of Glenfiddich and other fine Scotch whiskeys)